YOU
ARE WHAT YOU
BELIEVE

Lois B. Mayette

Author's Tranquility Press
ATLANTA, GEORGIA

Copyright © 2024 by Lois B. Mayette

All rights reserved. No part of this publication may be reproduced, distributed or transmitted in any form or by any means, including photocopying, recording, or other electronic or mechanical methods, without the prior written permission of the publisher, except in the case of brief quotations embodied in critical reviews and certain other noncommercial uses permitted by copyright law. For permission requests, write to the publisher, addressed "Attention: Permissions Coordinator," at the address below.

Lois B. Mayette/Author's Tranquility Press
3900 N Commerce Dr. Suite 300 #1255
Atlanta, GA 30344, USA
www.authorstranquilitypress.com

Ordering Information:
Quantity sales. Special discounts are available on quantity purchases by corporations, associations, and others. For details, contact the "Special Sales Department" at the address above.

You Are What You Believe / Lois B. Mayette
Paperback: 978-1-964037-36-3
eBook: 978-1-964037-37-0

Contents

Acknowledgement 1
Preface 3
Thinking the Powerhouse 5
Physical Health 47
Techniques for Reducing Stress 54
Death and Dying 57

Acknowledgement

Reading is a very important part of my growth and development. I read not so much for new learning but for what I call confirmation or affirmation. On my journey I learn through my spirit guide and because I am a doubting Thomas, I need to have proof that I am on the right path. So, books have been given to me at the right time as needed. It has been an awesome experience for me. One female friend gave me books like clockwork for over 10 years. She was also a reader and writer but how she knew what books to give me next was a mystery to us both.

Since I am a mental health therapist most of this knowledge was kept to myself. Colleagues were certainly not on my page and trying to share my experiences with them was not advisable. I did try to get them to think out of the box, but who was I.

I tell this not to be critical but to show how it is hard to move beyond culture and think for yourself. So here are some authors who kept me company.

First the most important reading is the Bible.

Dr. Bernie Siegel,

Father Powell

Dr.AM Krasner

Stanislov Grof

Wayne Dyer

Deepak Chopra

Betty Edie

Caroline Myss

Jeane Dixon

Nancy Wilson Ross

Stephen Lewis and Evan Slauson

Dan Brown

Sylvia Brown

Frank Tipler

Neale Donald Walsch

Since I read up to 50 books a year this is just a few remembered but they will lead you to the others.

I acknowledge my family most of all, both parents, siblings and my own children all who have taught me much.

Preface

I am what I believe as everyone is and we will believe it until it no longer serves us. My beliefs have changed greatly in the last several years. Namely the beliefs around my humanness. My body, mind and spirit approach to life has made for the changes. Who I am and what God is?

We are both spirit or energy. I am a human being which makes me different than God but only because I am heavier in this body and not as free as he/she is. I am a spiritual being having a human experience. I want to explore with you the real self and how to get in touch with the real you. The difference between the ego self and the real self. Some of which you have uncovered already no doubt but much that might be yet to be discovered. It is a journey that is exciting or it should be exciting. Culturally we have not been taught to enjoy the peeling away of the layers of the ego to finding the true self. When I speak of culture here, I am referring to the United States in general as we are a young culture and have been very exclusive in our ego centered concepts. We are adolescence at our best and are in much need to grow to the next phase of our being. After adolescence is community, now we were founded on community as the Pilgrim's left England because they did not feel free to Be, in that community. I am of Pilgrim decent and may have come full circle in this journey, a little ego maybe there but I can at least hope.

So what makes the individual grow or the culture grow? The direction that we are going in no longer serves us, change comes through outside forces or inside unrest. My take on what one I choose has been to go willingly for the most part to the waters rather than to be forced. If it comes from within it is willingly and if it comes from outside it is forced upon.

Each experience is a teacher and you need to be willing to grow or learn so not to have to repeat the experience over and over. We in the US are being forced to change as we placed our importance in the material which makes us adolescence. In order to move to a higher level of development we need now to see we are all one. What happens to one of us happens to all of us. We need to be a community again in the real sense. Many are already aware of this but the majority needs to understand how to get there from here.

Thinking the Powerhouse

Thinking is the powerhouse so if you change your thinking, you change your feelings and your behavior. Everything goes back to thinking.

A female friend and I were talking to a male one day and he called us bitches. It caught me off guard and my friend saw my shock of being called a bitch. After he had left, she turned to me and said, "Do you know what you just did?" "What", I said. "You reacted when he called us a bitch, do not you know what BITCH stands for?" Then she told me, "Babe in total control of herself. "I laughed and laughed and wrote it down and never recoiled again. I went on to teach others the definition of bitch. No more sting or power over.

The most powerful of ills in our culture are the labels we give persons. The danger is that they become their label stopping them from becoming all they can become. This is very destructive.

I teach that you are not your disease or label, but I always feel that I am swimming upstream against the current. I try to teach that they are not their label and to use what else is there. Once they and others identify them as the label then it is hard to get them to see they are more than that label. I hear well-meaning parents use the excuse for a child doing one thing or another as their label. The tragedy here is that self-esteem is greatly eroded and we all are affected.

My son thinks he was dyslexic in his early years and I say, "aren't you glad you did not know?" My point is that he did not limit himself and pulled out of himself everything possible. He went to college and is a very successful hydrogeologist. I have parents that introduce their child, "this is my she/he is Asperger or ADHD "or some such thing. It should be what you have not what you don't have. Teachers and doctors should be taught this in school as well as parents. Institutions gain from labeling and now it is backfiring on us. If we loved each other more we would drop the labeling of anyone. We lose the potential of that person and it affects all of us.

I went to a one room school house and I remember the teacher standing at the blackboard, being sure that we got the difference between the b and d and the g and q and etc. Where have all the good teachers gone that knew it was hard to differentiate between these letters, and she never mentioned a label. I was so blessed to have had that kind of teacher and education. Most of us could skip the eighth grade as we had heard it by then and knew it. We had 8th grade regents at that time. I must confess that I did not skip the 8th grade as going to the big high school for the tests took me out of my comfort zone and I could not concentrate. The teacher was shocked but was able to tell me what happened. Labeling can keep us in our comfort zone and not take healthy risks. Being conservative, is fear of the unknown and wanting to stay in the comfort zones. There is no progress in the comfort zones. Risks must be taken in order for growth to take place.

Two days ago, a 22-year-old male shot Congresswomen Giffords in Arizona. They want to label him mentally unstable. Know why? It relieves everyone of any responsibility for his behavior.

We had just come off the worse campaign, with behavior by supposedly adults running for election that made my toes curl. I watched very little TV for two months, it was so bad. And I chose to watch Canadian TV when I did. I went to Vienna, Austria on Sept. 2 thru 10th and had good conversations with the people there and they were honest about their socialist government as they stated that they never had it so good. They said it was hard to relate to the United States for our beliefs were not understandable. We talked about our being stuck but what struck me was I was there in 1990 and 1992 and had the same conversation with a couple of females in Munich, for three hours. They are very amazed at how narrow our thinking is and I could not say, there was one thing to disagree with. I think everything happens for a reason and I feel I needed to see how we are viewed by the rest of the world. Our behavior is adolescence as we think we have the answers for everyone, when we take care of our own very poorly. Our thinking is primitive and cave man mentality with just more expensive clubs. I heard that someplace and loved it. And since it is at the so-called top of our government that is so irresponsible where do those at the lower levels go for sound examples. Young adults in our country are having a difficult time making sense of the so-called adult behavior and do not have the maturity to deal with the contradictions. When I was growing up, we had much to take pride in and today it is fast been eroded. Limiting our terms in office of our elected official is one way of getting back on track as special interests and all those riders on laws will be less likely to have as much impact. We need to replace fear for love... Congresswomen Giffords was love according to the news. Arizona is Republican and she was Democrat so it leaves me to wonder what this young man that shot her had heard during the election campaign that affected him with such animosity. If he is mentally ill then maybe most of us are. Let's do something we have lost sight of, and become accountable.

We need to revisit here what I have said earlier about moving from adolescence to community; what happens to one of us affect all of us. It is an illusion to think any different. We are all responsible for what he did.

Start with your illusion of "you made me do it", statement. No, you are choosing to do it, feel it and believe it. Responsibility is lacking in adolescence but necessary learning. No one really has power over another, it is an illusion to believe that you do. Parenting is a wonderful experience as it teaches parents that they have no power over their children, lest the child gives them that power thru what I believe is fostered by respect. Fear is more than likely used in parenting but is not the true technique to be used, as we earn respect. Just being a parent is not necessarily a guarantee for respect. Again, you earn respect in parenting. The power over does not exist, lest earned. Talk about cultural changes that would take place if the belief of power over were dropped.

Most of my psychotherapy is just that trying to get persons to believe that they are giving away their power over to the event, persons, or situations. Just start to believe otherwise and you will be empowering yourself. Feels good!

What you resist, persists. Now stop resisting taking charge of your beliefs and change them. The more you pay attention to something the more it persists. Take the headache, it is there and when you get busy it is no longer there and you wonder where it went. Well, it was not getting any attention so it decided to get lost!! You actually cut off its focus and oxygen, so to speak.

In fact, in pain management, it is a good technique to focus intensely on the pain and back off, three times and pain goes away. Same principle resists and persist, only the other way around.

Everything is energy or it is nothing. It is all in your head! It is energy.

I am reading, "Soul Print", by Marc Gafne now and it is really worth reading. He is a modern day, Rabbi. It is more of a confirmation read than new information but he is telling it from a different perspective. It is important to see things from a different angle as it implants and verifies concepts more in your being. Remember practice, practice, practice. You can know something and not be able to use it in your being. So the more you confirm that it is a belief you want, the more it will become likely part of you. It has been said, that there is 18 inches between the head and the heart so it takes time for things to sink in and to be used with understanding. It is part of the process of becoming all you can become. Head is the intellect and the heart represents ownership of the belief and being able to use it.

When we look at others, we need to keep in mind that we are all one and we are all capable of the same thinking and behavior. "There but by the grace of God goes I". When you think differently, you feel differently and you behave differently. Thinking and believing are the powerhouse. Grace here means help form God, God does help us when we are ready or ask for help and are ready for the learning or remembering. Your readiness is a very important key here.

Spirit will not punish you to get you to learn. It is all up to you. We have consequences for our behavior and choices. We hear people say that God is punishing them and that is not true. There are consequences to choices. You made the choices and you earned the consequences. When you discipline your child, you are not causing their pain, they are in the choices. Good parent knows this and do not say that this hurts me as well as you. You might as well not discipline as you just took the responsibility away from the child. Get rid of a punishing God. God or Spirit is unconditional love.

What about miracles? Well, they do happen but it is likely that are more about the unknown and are built into the cause and effect ratio but we have not figured them out yet. It is still some of the mysteries of the world yet to be discovered. Awareness was the key to my out of body experience. I needed to be aware that my spirit leaves my body. Spirit leaves the body while we sleep and can at other times also. My seeing my life pass before me was the awareness that I can hook into the Akaskic records which have our life tree or records. Think of these records as all knowing about all of us. Awareness can also be thought of as consciousness. Your consciousness increases as your process in knowingness. Remember I was stuck for 15 years in churches, I knew this consciously but did not move on it I changed my belief as the church as a foundation. Like the born-again experience is just the beginning of a passion for the truth or Christ in us. The passion will fade if you do not fill it with new understanding. When I came home from church in the end and rewrote the sermons, the light bulb went on and I realized I need to move on. I wanted here to say I moved ahead but the words we choose are important as there is no ahead, as there is no right or wrong or no ahead or behind. You are not ahead, you are Still. Isn't that marvelous! You are STILL. Be still and know that I am God. Be still and know that I am Lois. Wow! Still as in Being. NOW all that is.

As a culture we seem to look backwards or forward but if NOW is all there is, then we are not living but just existing. Smell the roses. Live in the now. The projection that we do keeps us stuck and unhappy as it is always not present. Train yourself to be in the present moment and not think so much about yesterday or tomorrow. Can not change yesterday and let tomorrow take care of itself. At least wait for it to come to be able to do something about it.

It is the same about loving self, do it today not when you get the career, lose weight, or have a partner. If you love yourself now, the rest will just happen and your faults as you see them will fall away. That's the magic of life. I have what I need right now. Stop the wish list, stay in reality and enjoy the moment. Most depression is caused by wishing things were different but not wanting to make them different. If you do not want to move to the jobs because it would take you out of your comfort zone than that is ok but take responsibility for that. When you are out of work and look for a job you feel better as it feel like progress. Moving forward is in the now, not yesterday or tomorrow, do something good for yourself today. Action is needed now, so clean the garage, the closet, or kitchen and it will help you get off the pity pot. Change your thinking, believe in yourself and go inside not to others. Do you realize that changing your thinking changes the chemistry of your body? Yea, those stress hormones, those happy hormones and after a while they start to be more dependable. That is, they become more of your norm. They become elevated in your system on a regular basis. You are what you believe. I have not been to a doctor for 40 years and have not had a cold in 15 as this is my norm and it is programed into my Being.

Here is a theory I have about myself. I have lived many many lives, as I believe in reincarnation.

Probably 700plus, so learn easily some things as I have been there before. The spirit knows! I am aware as in de ja vu but mine is more in the recall and thinking area. Now do not take this to the bank as I said it was a theory, and all thinking is just that a theory to be expounded upon later. Do not get stuck in the box. We must see that we are always increasing our awareness of any topic. The verbal language especially English is limited, so we need deeper meanings or ways to express concepts.

The spirit in you or around you is God. God the all-knowing. God is everywhere. God is energy. Thoughts are energy. We are all one, all this I know has been said before but if we could get this what a difference the world would be. There would be no wars and conflicts would be waged by our higher self with negotiating in favor of everyone. Wow!! What a concept. Higher evolved human beings already do this either in their private lives or their public. Christian really need to look at what it means to be Christ like. This is an observation not a criticism. What observation?

War, killing my brothers and sisters since we are all one. Politics in the US, selfish and corrupt. Economics which states there is not enough and leads to hoarding. Love is lacking in all of these concepts. Take your own inventory now and see where you are since the only one we change is self. It really does begin with Me. Good news, more are beginning to get this, that love is all there is.

Love is consciousness so is a choice. We are insecure because we are adolescence, selfish, and self-centered but a lot of this is about to change. We need to choose love which is positive energy and if you will God. This is the ingredients for happiness. You think our economy is bad now, the worst is yet to come. History repeats itself until we get it right. The middle class got hurt the most in 2009 but that did not help those at the top to learn a lesson, so it is time that the top got their lesson. Sometimes we just out smart ourselves, ask any adolescence and they can tell you what is wrong with accuracy in the US. In adolescence it is all about me, and then you realize how and what helped you get where you are and you start to include others in your life. You can see how easy it is to get stuck here. It is nice to be the center of the universe. So just as individuals have to go inside to change things so does the society or culture. There is really no one to blame but self.

Blaming just prolongs the inevitable. If something has happened, accept it and move into the solution as blame keeps you dead in the water. You can only change self. Greed and corruption can only sustain itself for just so long and then it is bound to backfire. Band-aids will not do when a tourniquet is needed. Doing the wrong thing for the wrong reason will always bury us. We need to be doing the right thing for the right reason. Wisdom and common sense must prevail, not special interests. If I say I am love and do hateful things than it will come back to haunt me. Remember what goes around comes around or you reap what you sow.

We in the US have been a patriarchal society for too long as males have become insensitive to right and wrong. Big egos have become even bigger rather than the purpose of life is to reduce ego and drop adolescence. When you do the right thing for the right reason your gut tells you by your having the peace that passes all understanding. Alcoholic men are on the increase as they try to drown out the gut talk. They do not like themselves as they have become big con artists. Women have been asking for years, "Why do men lie, even when they do not have to go there?"

One reason is this insensitivity. Men believe it is only a lie if they are caught in it, otherwise it is a very cleaver move. They air on not getting call out for it. Transparency is now a buzz word but a good one, we may get there. I am an adult and do not like secrecy, as it is usually a downfall.

Example:

In good parenting the key is no secrets. I learned this 40 some years ago when I was raising my children. You try to find a way, age appropriate, to tell the truth about what is happening or did happen. The children will understand and be better for it. It teaches the children so many good principles. Not just honesty but feeling good in the gut. They will not hold sickness in the gut but will learn to check the gut for the truth.

Somewhere else in the book is another example of the Bush administration and his secrecy policies. which I think got us disliked around the world and is why we are falling now. WE cannot blame others as we were all in this together. We let it happen. Sometimes we just do not see the trees from the forest. Of course, fear was used and worked with the Bush administration.

Shame on us!

The truth is we have very little of the truth as we should never believe we know much as there is so much to know. We should always be open to new understanding and study all our lives not just after we get the piece of paper of accomplishments. Like a lot of accomplishments, it is just the beginning, so reading and studying to keep up with new thinking is essential. I am aware that it is fun for me and can be overwhelming for others. What to believe and who? It really does not matter as lots of reading is just theory or food for thought. You usually know what is for you and what is not. So give it a try. I read about 50 books a year and most of them are for affirmation and I get them in many strange ways. That is fun for me.

Story!

I recently met a woman, who went to Tulene University and I asked her if she knew my most informative professor and author, "Frank Tipler?" His book titled, "The Physics of Immortality" was a hard book for me with no physic background, so I have read it twice and still study it. I got this book in a second hand book store in Minneapolis, Minnesota. I am still in gratitude and awe as it was just the book, I needed to help me understand relativity and Einstein physics.

Information is not always coming from others as it is also be formulated with the individual. It maybe a nagging of sorts about something in your mind that keeps coming to the surface. Do not underestimate these thoughts. To grow you must pay attention to them as your learning like in schools are a progression. You are being encouraged to search out the idea. Physics kept coming up in my readings so I had no choice but to study what I could understand on my own. Much of my learning has been that way. If something does not ring true for you, do not dismiss it but ponder it further. In college I had problems with some of the concepts being taught and now know they were not good teachings. Some professors were ok with the questioning of these concept and some were not. The authorities of today will not be the authorities of tomorrow if we are to expound with growth and understanding. Everyone needs to be open to new understanding in their field. No thing is static as everything is evolving. Some people get their degrees and never open another book so they are stuck in old teachings. Everything is out there for the challenge. Be a free thinker. Go outside the box.

The books I read are three fourth affirmation. That means I already know or are in the knowing when I read them. The thoughts and ideas are formulating inside with the open door, you need to be open to growing. It is easy to say, "I do not like to read." There are talking books and etc. today so no excuse. Meditate and thoughts will come. I am a doubting Thomas so out of the blue books would be given to me by someone and they would be just as I needed them. This was so awesome and still blows my mind. The universe wants to give you the desires of your heart, someone said. That is a hard concept when you look at your life or around you.

Example:

Stay with my learning, understand I was doing my part of being open to the universe for my learning, I was at this point and needed more input and it was given.

Surprise, surprise! I should not have been surprised as it happened time and time again but I was always in awe.

So what are desires of the heart that the universe gives or honors? It is not something that will stop your growth and development. You do that without the universes help!! So when you feel that God is not listening, he may just be waiting for you to become aware to the fact that you do not need that or that it is not in your best interest. We are thinkers and created that way so do not try to pull the wool over God's eyes as he is the all-knowing. My having a deep desire to learn and know is what the universe sees and acknowledges is good for me. It is not just good for me but good for those I come in contact with. So we might say it is a pure desire. It is not self-serving only but always remember the I is very important. It is not selfish, lazy, prideful, arrogant, or destructive. As you get more in control of your thinking or rather get it under your control more, you will recognize pure thought. Our phase of materialism usually has to be processed to clean up thinking but materialism is necessary for many to go through. In materialism we ask for things of want rather than need. Wants do get answered for some as they may be in the stage of needing to know that it does not bring happiness. If I want a million dollars and it will ruin my growth, then I hope the universe ignores my request. No is an answer. If we are answered before we ask then once asked, we should then just hold it in our heart. Being persistent has its place but children, who are do not always get what they want nor should they.

There is no wrong or right to thinking and you will change it when it no longer serves you, and that is the way it should be. We have learned to respond to our situations from our past or experiences of the past. So old habits die hard, but the good news is that they can change no matter what they are or how long you have done it that or this way. You need to believe this in order to change and it is a choice as well as in your control. Spirit comes to earth in us to experience itself or God in our experiences. Not just good experiences but all of them. How we handle them and why. If spirit is all knowing than why the need to experience through humans? Did you ever want to relive an experience again and again? That is the experience of happiness, joy, peace, and love. Well spirit loves to feel our experience of remembering or learning. It is great joy when we uncover the truth for spirit as well as for you. You know how it feels to give to others and the joy of happiness in others, well you just produced more positive energy. It is all energy and we need to fill the universe with that positive energy, which is pure love. Love is all there is and needed to change the world.

Since love is all there is, then to grow and learn we must get rid of ego to move to pure love and that is the goal of our lives. The idea that likely kept us stuck for so long has been in the belief in reincarnation. It is important that you know knowledge is power. You might have always known, as I did, that one life to get it all RIGHT was a little ridicule but kept it under your hat. If others were not talking about it than you better not. Well in my practice clients were wanting to explore it more and more. I did a study on it and realized where it got squashed in the Christian belief, during Constantine's reign. The church wanted to get the peasants to come on board of the catholic church, so many of their beliefs were squashed and condemned as reincarnation was. Christmas has another interesting history. Christ was likely born in September. I will leave that for you to explore.

Reincarnation just always makes sense and you do not have to go but to look at nature to reinforce the ideas. Read Matthew 17:1-13. It was that the disciples and Jesus believed in reincarnation. What is the Second Coming belief? If Jesus comes again, will it not be the reincarnated Jesus? So if you believe Jesus was coming again you are believing in reincarnation or what else would you call it. These are the areas that we need to be exploring in order to learn and grow. I do not believe the bible is the last say, as God is moving us ahead not keeping us stagnant. If we take nature as our example, you see it moving ahead and so does the human race.

Many do not like the word evolving but we are in body, mind and spirit.

Ask yourself why you believe what you do and unlock the blockages. Remember we really know very little as there is so much to know. Speak to God as you would speak to anyone, the best prayers are those that are just talking and opening up to spirit, energy or God. If you are not following your intuitions and nagging's than you may be missing growth thru the spirit. Some are afraid of their own judgements so the self-doubt keeps them stuck. Yes, you do have to go out on that limb by yourself as you are a unique individual and what is waiting for you is different than the others. You can see why it is important to process a good sense of self in order to be ok out on that limb by yourself. Being comfortable in your own skin is the most important part of growth and development. It is not about what others believe it is about what you believe and how you operate from that belief. If something irritates you do not just dismiss it but start to examine why you are irritated. I will bet if you study it some you will uncover some new understanding about it and yourself, that is the way spirit or God works. These are the nagging's that I talk about. How else would God reach us? We really need to go inside not to others as the authorities for us.

I really try to focus on how to help our culture to move ahead or those that I come in contact with on a daily basis. So in 2005 when I predicted the fall of our economy I did not see how it was going to affect the whole world. Our economy affects the whole economy. I think that was what I had to learn how we have moved to becoming a one world as predicted. It must become that way, like it or not. We are really getting closer to we are all one concept. We are interdependent.

With mass media we know much, right when it happens or shortly thereafter. Years ago, we could say what we don't know will not hurt us but now we know better, what happens to one happens to all of us.

I watch very little television but still know what is going on as someone will tell me even if I do not want to know. We are sometimes taking the media as the authority, when it can be just to much drama. Adolescence loves drama and the US is adolescence and loves negative drama best.

Many are saying they too do not watch much TV as there is nothing on but sex and violence and even sport is violent. Sports maybe the last hurray for the male before they evolve into a more amenable community-oriented person. Have any of you had the experience that I have with commercials? They have put about eight in two minutes and for me it is funny how it is hard to realize that one has ended and another has begun for a second. Economy has driven our culture for too long.

What should drive our culture? Not money! You cannot take it with you when you go so why would you think it should be your goal? So what do you take with you when you go? When processing self, ask the right questions or ask the question differently, may be a better way of saying or thinking it as there is no right or wrong. It is where the heart is and if your questioning is for a pure reason, it will not really matter how you ask. I am trying to clarify here that the motive is more important than words, and motive speaks louder than words. Where the heart is the spirit is.

Love is all there is, so that is what you take with you when you die. All the love you have shown others, places and things. Real love conquers all. We will become more united by being concerned for everyone as your brother or sister. Community should be the driving force. Use manpower rather than money power.

We want everyone to be like us as if we have something everyone should want and why would they want adolescence? That is what we are in the US at our best. Democracy we do not have as we have to many laws and restrictions to be a democracy now. Can we return to a democracy? Yes, we can but we will have to process death and dying issues and stop trying to save everyone form their selves. Even God gave us free will. Ponder that for a minute for too many laws is not free will or freedom.

Adolescence always think they know it all and everyone want what they have. Therefore, adolescence is afraid of losing what they have. One sure way of losing what you have is to be afraid of losing it. The outside forces are the issue as the losing will come from within, it always does. The weak link is within. Russian communism ended from within, Egyptian culture is changing from within as is the rest of the Middle East. Transition is always difficult as change is not wanted by some who still want the same old and fear change, not wanting to think out of the box. We are always progressing in change as there is always a silver lining after the dust settles. One way of accepting change is to see it as not losing something but gaining more. Or sometimes just waiting to see how it all will plays out with interest.

Some say well it was good for yesterday, so it is good for today. There is a generation gap that is real and once you begin to see the gap you realize that that is because we would not grow if there was not the need for a gap. It is really the gage for growth. I could not stay an infant or a teenager and etc. so it is with cultures and nations.

Love is all there is so air on the side of love and realize that doing the right things for the right reasons is love. What is love? Love is a consciousness and a conscious choice. Love does not always feel happy or is love always just a feeling. There are hardships in love as well as sacrifices, but with hardships and sacrifices there will be a sense of doing the right thing, therefore a giving love feeling. Love is more than an emotion as doing the right thing absent of emotions will likely be best done without an emotional attachment. Emotions can get in the way of feelings. Emotions can be the out-of-control part of feelings, less emotions and more feelings. More balance to the thinking and feeling aspect of decision making. Love does not get reduced with less emotions at all as it likely increases and feels better as we are more in control. Emotions change the physical more so true feelings are overshadowed. Both feelings and emotions are physical but can be unbalanced. Rational thinking is necessary ingredient in separating emotions and feelings. Counting to ten maybe a good technique to slow down emotions and let feelings be more in control. Take charge of the emotions. Females are less emotional these days as they have taken more of a charge of their lives and more in control of their emotions. They are still very strong feeling persons. Compassion might be the better word. Males need to get in touch with these aspects of themselves as culturally we have squashed those aspects by not wanting them to seem weak when showing emotions. Little boys should cry and the same as little girls. It is the parents that do not like crying. Since we are created with both male and female traits, we are on planet earth to develop both traits. I was a tomboy when I grew and seem to think I needed to be as good as the male friends in sports and I was. I consider myself to be quite androgenous. What I mean by that is that my first thought about anything is not a male or female trait. I do not separate it in gender roles or jobs. Yet I love being female and feminine. I love being sexy and being masculine at the same time. I believe that perhaps both keep us physically and younger.

It takes many limitations out of play. Androgenous is a goal to be strived for in being the best possible person you can be. John Wayne was a turn off for me but Paul Newman a turn on. Look at what I am saying, to know oneself is to be in touch with feelings and it is not about the bedroom or lust. It is about energy. What kind of energy do you pick up in the situation. Love is a choice, a consciousness. The example is that Paul was a choice over John. We make those choices all the time and should be more aware of them and why. Make choices with more awareness.

Now feelings can lie to us. Emotions and feelings need to be combined with thinking or the intellect. Feeling can lie as in you may feel sad for no reason, you may feel someone is upset with you for no reason, and you may have fears about something that will never transpire. Worry is our biggest waste of time and energy. Be concerned but do not worry. I believe women worry and are sometimes proud of it as they think it is love. No thing to do with love. That does help them let go of it. Worry changes the chemistry of the body and can produce depression and anxiety. Concern will affect the body in a very mild way and will not do as much harm to the body. Worry is usually a control issue. Deal with the control issues and love issues and you can stop wasting energy in worry. You bring to you what you resist or fear is another good reason for letting go of worry. There is also a neediness in worry: a need to be important to persons, places or things. This does not mean that you cannot have desires but be sure you have control or not over the situation. If it is not in your control let it go. Prayer is a good tool to use here. Give it up to the universe or God. "Let go and let God," said the bumper sticker.

Think of worry as energy and the kind of energy you want others to receive. Work on trust issues as that is a big factor in worry. Charge the energy around you with positive energy. It is said that feelings are the language of the soul. What feelings? Love, trust, joy, and peace, not negative ones.

The soul is not emotional, yet feel what you feel knowing what is the real feeling needed. That is why you get unrest in situations. If everything is energy or it no thing, then surround yourself with positive energy. That is why we should take persons that are negative in small doses for they will suck your energy away.

Awareness takes the ego out of play so the real self, the knowing self can come forth. Awareness is calming, secure, positive, assuring, and peaceful. It is those soul feelings of love, joy, and peace.

One of my most vivid experiences with a teaching on awareness was driving home for three hours, two weeks before my daughter of 31 died of cancer. She was in such pain and did not want to be heavily medicated for her family's sake. She was still mobile and functioning at getting around as she also hated bed pans. I was angry and sad and was doing my usual tantrum: my being determines to get answers state. I said, "So much for love and detachment, why love to have to detach?" The voice in my head said, "It is not about detachment, it is about awareness." Ok, there it was again, that word, awareness. Spirit had been teaching me about awareness for some time. Feelings changed immediately to calm and serene. I meditated on awareness. It was really a high on life experience. The best explanation I have is that you are in spirit and not flesh at the time. I drove home in "total awareness" and it was timeless: a just being experience. I had surrendered to what is. It is awesome. Two weeks later I had some experience when I drove home after her death. I was the only one with her when she died and awareness was present. When I had discovered she had passed on, I started to cry and then I remembered awareness and in seconds I stopped to calm and peace. Detaching is what flesh does and awareness is what spirit does. Awareness a surrender to what is. It is the peace that passes all understanding. It is a state of acceptance, it is positive and no resistance. It is just Being.

We focus most of our life on doing and it is really about being. Being in the moment and not in the past or future. Want to know why we progress so slowly? We are usually in the reaction mode with the past or future dictating. Re-action is our mode. You are not re-creating in re-action mode. Our baggage keeps us in our defense mechanisms from our past. We hold on to old wounds and react from them. Again, we are what we believe and our beliefs are formulated usually by our experiences as experiences are our teachers. Our experiences are not right or wrong or good or bad, they are just our chance to learn and grow. Try to stop labeling them and see them as just there to teach.

If your reaction is not serving you then change your reaction. There is justifiable anger but the rest is a waste of time and energy. Anger is a good motivator so use it with less energy expended and go for the changes it can produce. Change reactions. At lease do not make a new law for everyone else to follow as it may be just the experience they need to learn and grow. Back to what we are if too many laws, we are a totalitarian government. We have taken away individual decision making for laws. Now here is the kicker, we have become more lawless, rather than lawful. Really what we fear is what we bring to ourselves as an individual as well as a nation.

We become irresponsible not more responsible as we become poor thinkers. What was communism? It was not really a bad idea but left many without any say, so it got top heavy.

Holding things in common was not wrong or right but just left no room for growth. So it is with a totalitarian government. We hate the word socialist but it too has its place as the government holds or owns everything. It can be the best of times or the worst of times. As growth is not there also. Democracy is the way to go but you cannot have all the decision making by laws. Again, no room for growth. Let me make up my mind who and what I want to be. If we saw death and dying in a different light, we would not be trying to save everyone from themselves. Now I do see death and dying in a different light and I will address that in the next chapter.

To give an example of how too many laws foster the opposite that we think it would be in parenting. If we give them to much as in things or thinking we produce children who do not know how to make decisions or be creative. They will lack drive and motivation. They also seem to be looking for love and direction in all the wrong places. I find that lets say, 20-year-old. They know what is. They know they do not want that. But they have no clue as to what to do or how to make a difference. They lack good decision-making skills and that is why students from other countries can surpass them in the same classroom. We have dictated for too long what to think and how to think. Big problem with WASP. We may have taken ourselves out of the playing field. Parents today seem to be just surviving.

There are two kinds of people; the living and the walking dead. The living are those who create life and the walking dead let life direct them. The walking dead are tossed to and throw with little creative thinking. They are the ones loved by advertisements, our government and the medical professions. Do not think, just let us do it for you. Sheep to slaughter. No sense of ownership of living. Life is really what you make it and over half of our culture are the walking dead. It at the same time is changing and more are becoming aware. You really do have to set yourself apart to grow, not in isolation but in thinking. We learn the most in adversity. Different people, places and things or events are our teachers. Adversity gives us a change to change something. It can be as simple as changing how we view or think it. Did you ever realize that no one has it made, so to speak? Everything can become a rut or routine after a while. It is not meant to be static, so we need to be creative with life. Re-create yourself anew each day. Stay in the now and present moment. Do not look back or forward but in the present and what does this moment want or need. The process really works like this: the event or adversity is there to teach, now be creative with it. If it has been in your face before; re-think it and change your response. Do not keep using the same old tactics. If they even worked for a long time, it is time to change them when they decide not to work this time. That is the way the invitation for change works. See them as a challenge not as a problem as challenges will give you an option and feels more positive. It will motivate.

I had a little prayer at this time that I used for years. Please do not take this away until I have learned everything from it as I do not want to repeat it again. The message in this little prayer was that I wanted to grow. Do not say, "why me?" as the statement should be, "why not me?" Do you not want to grow? Be challenged? Be alive?

Insanity is described as doing the same response hoping for different results. Think with new options, it may have been good for yesterday but not today. Others may want to stay in the status quo but this is the place to set yourself apart and be creative. The universe is wanting us to see there is another way and it will seem foreign to us but it likely is creative. Do not want short cuts to growth. It is all you can really own and take with you when you die. Look at it as graduating from one stage to another. Not good or bad, right or wrong, it just is. A gain not submission. A surrender to what is will feel really peaceful and a deep sense of profound understanding or awareness. It is giving up one option for a broader option. As we gain more details about something we change the way we think and respond to it. We need to be remindful that we know very little as there is so much to know and the openness to growing is the prerequisite to growth. The meaning of life is to become all that you can become. Become creative, curious and thinking out of the box are your friends. The fear of being alone can stop us from being ourselves in growth as we fill our days with busyness. More people in our culture are learning to center down and listen to that still small voice. We do need to take time for ourselves. We are social animals and seem to think if we are not alone, we are loved, but loving yourself first is necessary. How do you get to know yourself if you do not take time to reflect on self. I use a technique that is called free association after asking myself profound puzzling questions. In doing that I feel I get to know why I responded the way I did in a situation and how to change it to serve myself better. Do you know, that many times I did not need to respond in a situation at all, when I did. That has been the greatest lesson. We change when we pay attention to our behavior and change that which needs changing. Having time to reflect is important. Change your thinking will change your feelings and your behavior. Thinking is the key to change. Stop asking others or situations to change as the only one you can change is self. Focusing on the wish list of others to change will just keep us dead in the water. It takes one person at a time to make a difference. That is the same as blaming others, it is a waste of energy. Others do not care or will change when they are ready.

Blaming stops you from going inside for the answers. It really does not matter where the situations began, it is more about how did we solve it. It is in your face to teach you something.

Do not waste time on blaming.

Who and what do you want to be in it all is the question that you should ask yourself. It just is, so now take the ten minutes to slow down our reaction time, clear our heads and decide from the NOW what is the appropriate direction. Do not let it come from the past but take it to a new level of the now. It is hard to break old reactionary tactics but well worth it it as growth will feel good. Each break through with changes in reactions will be a spiritual experience and therefore feel good. That is the key; feeling good. That is where it is said that the angels rejoice; a break through. These feeling are sharing, helping, caring and giving which are of the soul. When we die we will have feelings not emotions. Feeling are natural and emotion are chosen for experiences. We will let go of emotions which are part of feelings that may not be facts. The feelings that are being expressed here come from love. If feelings of love are the language of the soul than it is positive feelings not negative ones. Negative are our teachers and positive are verification. That is why the peace that passes all understanding comes after a good response to a person or situation.

It is the high on life feeling. I'm so glad to be alive feeling. Taking good care of yourself is priority as you have nothing to give away if you are not in a good place. Once you are in a good place you will want to give it away whatever it is. We are social animals for this reason as we cannot contain our happiness, it must be shared. Look at it as happiness spilled over. Happiness is a choice as feelings are a choice. Is the glass half full or half empty, your choice.

Old habits die hard so if you are inclined to say, "well that is just who I am", then you will stay right there until you no longer want too. It is your choice what you think or believe.

Here is a standard question; "Do you think humans are basically good?" The answer is a choice.

God does not make junk. Go to a hospital and look into the eyes of a new born, you will see differences, but good. How good does the touch feel to the newborn? Are the caregivers, relaxed, cheerful, loving or uptight, angry, sad and etc. Abuse at an early age can lead to a number of later dysfunctions, especially self-hate and anger. Everything is energy so new born's pick that up easily as they are very tactile at birth. New born's have little choices for understanding what is happening to them but the difference between our childhood and adulthood is the choices in processing what happened to us in childhood. It is really necessary to know oneself by looking back on our early experiences that we are aware of. You do not need to get stuck in them just look at what you took away from the experience and move beyond it to a strength that it might have given you or an awareness of it. The awareness is not just for you but likely for someone or something of the future. Maybe it becomes a strength for a teaching to others. This whole book is one of my experiences; both directly or that I have been made aware of by other's experiences. We are all trying to do the best we can and that may have limitations by our hurt and pain of experiences.

Just a few words on parenting since we have looked at new born's.

Marriage and parenting are the two hardest relationships in the universe. However, they are the ones that we grow the most in. They are big teachers and both require unconditional love. Unconditional love is doing the right things for the right reasons. When is helping hurting?

In parenting we are attempting to prepare the child for the big tough world out there. Fear is used to much in parenting and other institutions that the child will come in contact with in this culture. That is doing the wrong thing for the right reason. You want them to get good grades but conditions on it is not the way to go. Fear is used as a short cut for not being more involved in the process of helping them pull out their potential. In encouragement, they learn to trust themselves and it became who they are and it in and of itself will be a lasting trait for them. Conditional love is fostering a not measuring up trait. There is never enough, not good enough and self-doubt. Many of our disorders are developed here. Fear is the opposite of love.

Words we choose are important as they come with different connotations or baggage for people or culture. Language is all man made and so are its connotations. In the act of communication, it is important to clarify the meaning of the words you are using. I do not like the word marriage as it comes with a history of primitive concepts. Study its history in the world and you will wonder why we still use it. Helpmates, partners, or friends would do better as concepts right now.

The unequalness is a concept of marriage that is primitive as there is no unequalness, we are complimentary, which implies no unequalness. No one was ever intended to be power over another. Who gives these women in marriage is so primitive even if you adore your father for you are not property to be given away. I adored my Dad and I know he did not see me as property and those words were there as at the time I did not know better. I would do it differently today. So the change would be the connotation and words used. Language can be the most misunderstood in communication skills and that is why clarification is so necessary.

Telepathy is the language common to us all. It is the language of the universal mind or God or spirit world. Telepathy is from one mind to another mind. It is energy as thought is energy. God says he answers before we ask, as thought is done before the asking or saying or thought is faster than language. You think it first and it is out there no real need to say it. Psychometry is the history in energy of a place, item and etc. It is transmitted by energy or thought. Like telepathy, after you die it is the language and if you think it, it will appear. after a while you will start to control your thinking as it will get to be too much or enough. Why not do that before you die, so you can enjoy the wonders of the universe that you know nothing about. I scuba dive and enjoyed a wonder time exploring the reefs so my wish upon death is to sit on the bottom of the ocean and watch all of that universe go by. I was able to sit on the bottom in Marathon, Fl on the Keys and Palancar in Cozamel was 95 ft down and could not see the bottom so you just hung around.

I was 62 years old then and experienced that day of being one with everything. It was a total present moment - body, mind and spirit. The awareness was very keen, no fears or concerns but great awareness. I was one with the ocean, fish, and surroundings. It was a split moment but a vivid and powerful one. Thoughts were telepathic and ego was put aside. I write and do psychotherapy without ego much of the time so I am familiar with how to put ego aside.

It is a training like living in synchronization. You grow to get there. You start by believing there are no coincidences by using your intuition and honoring them. The more your exercise your intuition the more it increases. It is really faith, believing in something hoped for but not seen. Culturally we have been trained to believe if it is not seen or proven than it is not real.

We want proof of everything when really, we need to take back the mysteries of life and the spirit of life.

Maybe putting ego aside is a little misleading as ego is not as conscious as it is habitual. I do not say or think I am going to be intuitive, it is a state of Being. Getting out of ego into the mode of being. We are about doing rather than being. You learn who you are so you can be who you are.

The false self is put aside so the real self can operate more. The more you let it happen the more it will happen. It is like any habit. You must study, practice and believe to get there. Like the meaning of life is to become all you can become and it is a process, so is being intuitive a process.

You cannot fake it or hurry it, it will happen as you get to understand the mysteries of life and self. It is always awesome and never taken for granite. It is like an out of body experience, you cannot choose it, it just happens. Now it happens when you have done your homework so to speak. It takes you being on the journey to Being. It is thinking out of your box and to the spirit dimension into the mysteries of life. Mysteries today maybe the known's of tomorrow. It is that we do not yet know, not that there is not an explanation for them. Remember Jesus believed that we would do greater things than he did. What happened? We are not doing as much as he did.

We really have digressed. Over the years there has been healings, and what we call miracles but not wide spread. Churches were responsible for that as the preaching was power over rather than empowering. I really was in churches for 65 years and can tell you I may have felt good about going but did not feel empowered. It may have been the universes design for me as I was driven to explore the mysteries on my own. I am a doubting Thomas but really open to understanding.

I do not stop searching until I get the peace that passes all understanding. Maybe I am Thomas reincarnated. I am a thinker. The earth is not round so why do we still call it round? Black persons are not black but brown so why so we call them and they call themselves black? My thinking will go there without a struggle because that is who I am and, in a sense, groomed to be.

Books have been my partner for years in the form of affirmation. In the process of learning for me is the desire to understand, then the teaching or knowing and then the affirmation. It has always been awesome and mind blowing and never taken for granite. I needed proof that what I was thinking had some validity. What you know today may be valid for today and expounded on tomorrow. That is the fun of life. This may leave some discouraged because why bother if we really never have the truth. Well, the truth for today should be exciting. Relish in it as long as you like. You will change it or explore its further possibilities when it no longer serves you. We are a negative culture much of the time so many say they do not like this or that but still stay in the situation doing the same old. So recognize if you are going to change but do not. I stayed in the church 15years after I knew I was not getting anywhere. It is hard to give up what was. We grieve the loss of everything that changes but fail to see that embracing the new is going to be freeing. Much of our life is going to change why not embrace it rather than fight the inevitable. An example that I am experiencing now is ageing. It is only relevant if we make it so. All of this depends on your belief systems. Belief systems need to be realistic. If you worship youth and beauty, seeing it leave will be noticed. If you except what you were given and use the many ways to identifying yourself, you will not see the change as negative and be more excepting of the change. Try not to use words that indicate limitation with ageing. I really never paid attention to my age but this year, I started to use it in a beneficial way. Then I started to gage everything by my age and was not feeling that good about it. I was seeing losses. So stopped using it as a yard stick. If I started to focus on it then I could stop focusing on it and I did. Just that act was enough for me to get right on track and feelings changed. You can be realistic without making it a gage for everything. Relish what you have left not what you lost. If you worship youth start to the beauty inside rather than outside. It helps to tell yourself it is shallow to see the beauty outside as the real beauty is always inside. Let's groom the beauty inside so when it is time for ageing evidence that we are ahead of the game. It is always an advantage to be ahead of the game and it does take conscious thinking. I am glad that I am still learning and growing. Learning is really remembering and I really can relate to that as I am peeling away the layers to what is. It was always there for the discovery. There is nothing new under the sun. It all was, is and will be, as it is all energy. Like most energy, it may change its location and intensity but it remains. We die and leave the body and what remains is spirit, soul or energy. We become lighter in spirit as our bodies are heavy with material that does not have eternal life. Think of a tree, it is made of the same elements as we are in body. Cut the tree down and it is still the tree in different forms; fire wood, flooring, furniture, homes and etc. but its energy is still that of the tree. You might say that energy is the most important element of us and trees. There is a spirit of the tree and a spirit of the human that is all there is. We both also have physical energy and spiritual energy that are not really separate from each other. The tree likely has more energy value than humans because of trees diverse usage so respect the tree. We could not live without them and that should help with how we are all one. Humans were created last because of our need for everything else that was created before us. Vegetation and trees are necessary for our survival as pure as air is of great need in our survival. Trees provide us with oxygen so love the tree. Plant a tree.

A word about the physical energy as in exercise. Exercise brings in more oxygen into the body and that can help balance our feelings and behavior. Thinking becomes clearer as we put aside our ruminating thoughts and focus on breathing. Focusing on exercise and breathing will distract us and soon we feel more alive and less stressed. Clearing our heads give us the opportunity to see that things are manageable and solutions come forth. Exercise is essential for a balanced life. If you feel something is not right in your life, it is likely that you are not balanced and taking a holistic approach to living. The body needs exercise, the mind needs challenges and the spirit needs growth and development. A note about exercise, you may think that house work and career work is enough exercise but it does not have the value that exercise for exercise has. The reason is that the message to the body is not the same. When I exercise for exercise's sake, it is more about the message that says I believe I am a very important person who needs to respect that exercise it important to my well-being. It is the same for physical healing it is more in the mind and beliefs systems than in the physical healing. This is also a good example of how everything is dependent on everything else. We are all one. The spirit is the essence of you both known and unknown or your potential. Drawing out your potential is the most important part of your journey. To really live and not be the walking dead, you must go inside to know yourself, your potential as in who you want to be, and who you already are that is not evident yet. This again is a good example of remembering rather than learning as your potential was born in you. You are drawing it out or remembering. If it wasn't there or possible than you would not be able to develop it. To challenge ourselves in new areas is to see if it is something we'd like to be or do and have a talent there. We need creativity and curiosity to do that. Our schools have failed our children in this area. Schools are more about route learning than creative learning. We are asking the children to learn from the past and not think out of box. Technology today maybe activating one area of the brain but neglecting another.

"Tiger Mom", the book about tough love parenting was attacked by parents, likely who really felt their parenting skills were not adequate. We disagree more when we feeling the lacking in ourselves. It was of course taken out of contents as the children of the parent writing it stood behind the mom and so did her husband. Look more at the end product. Who is in charge these days? It does seem as the children are running the parents, not the parents running the children.

Parents seem to feel guilty for being less available for children when both work so give them things to make them happy and of course that is not what happiness is all about. Children need strong guidance today as they always did and children with strong guidance feel more secure. Their security comes from the parents' security. You can have no thing and still feel very secure. Children do not want to run the show. My parents were very strict and today I see how that was good for me and shaped the good in me. There is nothing wrong with limiting cell phone, TV watching, curbing sports and just hanging out. I stayed home for 19 years to raise three children and it was the best job I ever had. I did not have too, I chose too. I gave up a good job with Eastern Air Lines and would do it again the same way. It is not necessary or for everyone but it was for me. I did not get perfect children but they knew they came first and were loved. I was in a sense a strict Mom. Love makes the difference as my parents were love also and we had little in the material sense. Priorities were stated, followed and respected as the why's got answered. Their biggest problem today is dealing with angry persons who are taking it out on others. They say I did not prepare them very well for the real world. My favorite word was fun so if it was not fun, I do not do it. That made for a rose garden and a non-drama world. Everything is drama today. We are all perfectionists, which can be an asset or a liability. Mine is, I like to think in remission now for the most part. We have to get rid of the liabilities that no longer serve us and keep the strong points. It is the thinking that really is the powerhouse that changes the way we see things. A very powerful chapter in "Feeling Good" by Dr. Burns was Dare to be Average. You might say, "who wants to be average?" The fear of making mistakes is likely the root of perfection. Stop checking and rechecking everything for the fear of mistaken. Mistakes are learning growing experiences. If you are not making mistakes, you likely are not going anywhere. Take risks and learn and you are bound to make mistakes. It is all in the learning and having a good sense of humor about mistakes will help you take risks. Do not throw the baby out with the bath water, keep the strong points in perfection like good organizer, hard worker, through, and doing your best at everything without going overboard. Let go of the fear of making mistakes and make some.

We really want to learn as we are doomed to repeat our mistakes if we are not willing to grow. Interestingly enough I recently testified in a court custody battle. Notice I said battle. Well, that is what it feels like in a court room. The energy in there is not always positive. Some feel they are going to lose and some win. That makes it a battle for what they want. I tried to stay grounded or in spirit, if you will. It is not easy with that kind of energy darting all around. This is the best example of how we are one and what affects one affects others. All in all, I felt good about my role in it all. We are all on a stage and just players. It is all energy and collective energy is real. You are not an island unto yourself and will be affected by other's energy. Understand this helps when you feel out of sorts in a situation and cannot find out the reason for your feelings as it may not be about you at all. We are all connected as far as energy is concerned. Since I can feel energy more or more aware of it, it is fascinating for me. We say the vibes in the room were this or that, well what were you saying but the energy in the room was this or that. Paying more attention to it and not so much in your feeling is important in not missing the chance to see how energy and feeling operate. This situation asked me to stay focused on the questions being asked and not on the energy of others but to use my own spiritual energy in the positive. It is hard not to let ego get involved as it is so easy in these situations to let it. It is not just courts that this is evident but a lot of organization of competitiveness. Competitiveness is another big downfall in our culture. It really should be about doing your best not others. We have a strong need to compare, which does harm. Keeping ego in check is not easy as we are reactionary. We are defensive and in fact the place to start to grow is looking at your defense mechanisms. We react from our past experiences.

Even lawyers seem to be more subjective than objective as it is hard to be objective but fascinating non the less. This is a good example of how collective energy really works. The more people in a room the more subjective the energy. Intimacy is more likely to happen in small groups than in larger groups but even large groups intimacy will be there if we are all on the same page. This is how churches fire up the crowd with an hour of song and praise. It is also the fire for demonstrations. Advertising uses this concept to manipulate your energy. Energy does include emotions, feelings and thinking. Too much emotions will block thinking and rational emotions will not come through. Reducing the non-essential emotions are primary for staying in control when faced with difficult tasks or situations. This also leads you to knowing yourself more and is an ongoing journey. Self-esteem is so important and every person is a good person, just groomed by experiences. Some people have had a hardening of the heart and shut down too much from the experiences of life. We might say the heart chakra is closed. This happens when at an early age a person does not receive love or a sense of importance. Mom and Dad maybe alcoholics and into themselves or abusive. So the shutting down is to protect oneself from any more pain but likely they cause themselves more pain in not having dealt with it yet. People who shut down are usually very bright but lack healthy coping skills. Helping them process the hurt, pain and anger is not difficult. They need to be ready to give it up, which is the first step. Many have used the pain, hurt and anger as a way of life and it is all they know and it has become learned behavior.

Learned chaos is not uncommon. We change when it no longer serves us and all the preaching in the world is not the answer, it being ready to give old behaviors up. Thinking is the power house.

The US is adolescence at its best so therefore the drama of life is today's excitement. Chaos maybe excitement for some and the norm, learned behavior and boring without it. We tend to make a word negative when it maybe positive for others. The desk sign may say, "this desk may be disorganized but I know where everything is." To that person moving one thing makes now the desk unorganized. It can be neat to see it from another's perspective. We should try it more. This was a big step for me in growth as I am a perfectionist, hopefully in remission for the most part now. Love is all there is. Critical spirits are not included in love. Always in a situation ask, "what does love look like now" and do the loving thing. I love your chaos, disorganization and I am so glad that you are ok with who you are. There is not wrong or right as well as good or bad it is all relative. It is all about what you want or need and is different for everyone. We should allow for others to have their preference as well as be comfortable in our own. It is not necessary for you to change yours but just allow for more truths. Differences are our beauty. Each change when what they believe no longer serves them. Some people do not like happy people and some like to be poor me and resent anyone trying to take that away from them. Misery likes company, so let it be.

You will know you have arrived in a good place when how and what others are doing and being do not affect you. You will just do a lot of chuckling inside. That is the goal.

The real key to change is thinking so that the feelings line up with your reality now. The reality you have today will always being changing as more information is received. This should be exciting and the pace you grow should not be the issue, just the willingness to grow. If you were Christian and God was conditional love, if you were good whatever that was, then he approved of you. Truth, is he has to love you no matter what you do. You may have believed that God only loved Christians. How lame is that! All great religions at the core of beliefs, believe the same. Study them. Why would a creator not like what he created? He created us all. Changing your beliefs is not painful and most of them, the change that is, makes sense. If I created the world, I would love all of it not just part of it. It is so unique, so why do we want to visit as many foreign countries, as we do? The US is one of the youngest of developed countries and we act the part well. In adolescence we think everyone wants what we got, we think we have the answer for everything, and we are right. Wrong the differences are our beauty. It is true that all changes must come from within and they do in spite of ourselves. If change is done for others than it will not last. Inside individuals and inside cultures. People all over the world are wanting more control over their lives and are doing it from within, except when we war and want to force our beliefs on others, stating it was in their best interest. That is not Christ like, so where is Christianity in it?

Beats me! We need to leave them right where they are until they no longer want to be there.

What gets in the way of leaving persons to their own growth is expectations. We like to be validated so we push and shove people into our beliefs. Ever have someone shove the Bible in your face and tell you that you were going to hell, which there is none? That was so not Christ like. Their desire was just to be right. They wanted to have something of value. The only validation one need comes from within, validate self. Actions still speak louder than words. Reach out and help the one you like the least not as in enabling but giving them a new start. A good sense of self is so needed to validate self.

Now it is alright to speak your truth but have no expectations. The story about the seed falling on barren ground, rocky ground, and fertile ground. Let it go where it is meant to go with no expectations. Grounds here can and does represent persons. Some are ready and some are not and some may in the future be ready, or it is food for thought. In reverse if someone speaks their truth, listen ponder and see if there is anything of value for you in it. If you know yourself well then it will just take a split second to process it. If accused of something you did not do, no need to defend yourself as a rule, just state your truth. That will in and of itself take the sting out of it and have no expectations. Changing someone's mind that is already made up is usually a waste of energy. Most of our news is gossip so we like gossip and if that is where you are than start by not repeating anything but that which is firsthand information. News is so much drama, drama and not the news worthy or growth producing medium. More people are saying that they watch limited news as it is too much drama. I want to give a gold metal to the guy that exposed those secrets at Wik Leak. If you believe in eternal life than you would not have secrets or fears. Shame on us again. We will tumble from within, as history has taught us. There is no security, it is one of the first illusions you get to see as you process the self. Our uprising is yet to come but it will as Egypt and Libya and the rest of the Middle East. That is the way it works unless we go willingly to the water. In the US we have too much ego yet to go willingly. The fall is yet to come as the haves will not give up without a fight. Good news some of the haves like Gates, Winfreys, Buffets and a few have left their egos behind and see life differently, so share better. If you identify with money than you are likely insecure about money so there is never enough. If you identify with youth than when it is no longer there you become insecure. Money and youth are those identities that are sure to come and go. So check out your strong identity areas. Hopefully it will be or become something that does not flee like compassion, caring, concern, sharing and most of all love. You are in full control of these identities and ask yourself if this is who you want to be now. The last will be first after death is a clear example for changing your ways. Individuals do not give up their identities easily as groups do not and that is why change is so slow. Now with the economy so bad, look at all the organizations that agree something has to be done but no one wants it in their territory.

What I do for myself and others in advancing the soul or essence is what survives death. It becomes part of our DNA or genetics. We do not age as the beauty is now within and hopefully comes forth. It is not outside that counts but inside. It is important that we become more responsible for our own advancing of our soul. Think of programing your DNA or genetics and how that works.

Well, here is a laypersons version: Each time you come to earth you come to grow and develop. Develop what? Well, it is not your body, you leave that behind, however your body is important in the developing. A healthy body is part of the advancement when it comes to DNA and genetics for it is all energy. Let's say I abuse my body with drugs, alcohol, food and laziness. Now let's say I remember the body is a part of the whole and that I need to respect it and groom it as a stewart of a precious piece of the mysteries of life. What version of these examples advances the soul? It is that simple. Can you see in this example that only the advancements get counted upon death?

Spirit has no need to drag around negative energy. It will take only the positive growth plus your past lives' developments. So the soul or spirit leaves the body with the whole of learning and the programing of DNA and genetics. I am a product of all my past lives as well as all my ancestors past lives. We are all one. We are all energy.

Do not get stuck in language as it is man made and limited which can stop your understanding and growth. Get the picture that you came to planet earth to remember who you really are and who you want to be as well as what you want to advance at this life time. The Being is more important than the doing. The cost of advancing your soul is energy, spending energy to get energy. Increase your energy, aura or soul, as anything that is energy will survive death and go with spirit in eternal life cycle. You can kill the body but not the spirit. See I can picture all those people we have killed as a culture, in our wars today, going to spirit world. I know they were intended to die but only if we learn a lesson in their death as to how destructive wars are and how primitive.

There is no winning in war or fighting of any kind, please get this.

So spirit is always trying to move you ahead as it has a mind of its own and knowledge that you can tap into. Be willing to learn and grow. Get out of doingness and quiet down. Look at your fears when you are quiet. There is no need to have them. That is contained in the concept of eternal life. Nothing to fear itself.

Churches used fear and conditional love of God to control and have power over you. Now take back your power. Not all churches were as bad as others. My Methodist Churches were the middle of the road church so gave me freedom to explore and change. Still, I felt that it gave me historical Jesus and Christianity but not much on the mystical Jesus. The Christ to me is the spirit within us all and Jesus was a good example of the Christ within, not exclusive of other great leaders. So I say we do not follow Jesus as much as we follow The Christ in Jesus. The author of,

"90 Minutes in Heaven" sang songs he said in his out of body experience but they were not about Jesus, he found this puzzling but went no further in the book for exploring, why? In my out of body experience I also sang and no Jesus songs. My take now is that there are no elevated spirits that there are no favorites and Jesus like Buddha, Mohammad, Ghandi, and any of our great movers and shakers are showing the Christ within. We can arrive while on earth at a point where you know when spirit is operating and ego is absent. We failed to realize that it is said," to not make any other God's before me." Because flesh is flesh and spirit is spirit. We are all one. God is us and we are God. Blasphemy this is not, read your Bible it is there. Do not read the King James version of the bible, it is old language and antiquated. It is not how you talk, so get one that talks to you.

There is still a lot of mystery, mystique, and mysticism to explore in spiritualism. The unknown today will become the known of tomorrow and different for us all. Someone has to explore them and why not you. Setting yourself apart is necessary to have time to pray, read, study, ponder, and experience. Others in your journey are important as likeminded people will be encouraging and balance the feelings of being alone. However, we are all unique so our experiences will be different and that is important. It is differentness that tell you when you are the true self or ego. If you still need affirmation then that is ego.

Example: When you were a child, you were a student and needed to absorb everything. It was all belonging to others, this knowledge was history of others experiences and beliefs. As a young adult hopefully, you started to question what was important to keep as yours. (Schools lack this stage of teaching) This process was to continue into adulthood. We really need to take all that knowledge and look to see if it has any value for us as individuals. About one third of what I learned in six years of college, I have used or kept, the rest gave me confidence to question. The confidence along with the training to think was very important for the rest of my life. Some things we learn, we keep as learned and now ours, some things we add to or tweak to fit our lives and the rest we regurgitate and spit out. Spit out as it has no value in our lives but it may have value for others. In fact, I am convinced that there is a healthy generation gap as what worked yesterday is not meant to be for tomorrow or we would not grow. "Good old days" do not exist and is a myth. Creativity is an essential part of growth and the purpose of life. We are advancing when we are creative. I am afraid that we have many young children that are not creative as technology may help them be creative without using what important as needed in today needs.

Where you focus is important and what you are focusing on is key. Fighting the dragon is good as a game but 24/7 gaming is not the way to go.

We have all focused-on materialism and found ourselves neglecting other important things. Like our relationship with others. Usually bigger and better was the push. After materialism will come a need to be alone, to find self, the real self and let go of ego. Creativity is so needed here. According to the Hindu beliefs, the third stage of growth and development is going into the forest which sets you aside. The focus is getting rid of ego and learning all you can, not only for the self; the real self but the fourth stage is the wondering sage, which gives to others what you learned in the forest. Going into the forest to me is a beautiful analogy. This is a hard stage for many as this culture does not like to be alone or separated from the others. Now in the forest you will encounter likeminded persons to help you grow and test knowledge out with. The first stage was as a student and the second of the community. In primitive cultures (Ha Ha) the elderly were the archives of knowledge or the happy wonderers. Watch out to what you call primitive. Since we favor youth in this culture, you can see we may have a difficult time with this stage too. We are retarded to many cultures. We need to get back to honoring our elderly. I have learned a lot from the elderly that no text book ever mentioned. Youth would not want to get rid of ego as to them it would feel like giving up what they were just learning to enjoy. When the student is ready the teacher appears. Usually, the wondering stage phase is common sense smart. The wise elder. We will be very lucky (no such thing as luck) to find a wise teacher. I did not find one but I did find many. There are many very intelligent persons with no wisdom or common sense, so be careful of who you look to for guidance. Intellect can be full of ego and unable to think out of the box and have only what is someone else's experience's or knowing's. Dedication to being well balanced may seem like to much work and uncertainty but once you put the practice in motion it will become the routine that feels good. People who exercise each day find that one day without it feels like something is missing and it is. It is very fulfilling and you sleep better, eat healthier, and your focus is keener. You will be eating better as your focus will be on eating for the right reasons and not because you are bored or unhappy. More oxygen in our blood stream makes a different for body, mind and spirit. We become sharper and revitalized. It was not surprising that we became fat Americans. Technology is sedentary and the lack exercise along with snack foods being eaten without thought are part of the reason. Parental guidance was also an issue as we want our children to be savvy in all the new technology. Parent's loss control of their children in the 80's and early 90's and have not gained control yet. Do you remember when back there the courts and social agencies gave the right for children to emancipate their parents and were set up in apartments of their own and paid for by the tax payers? It was a crazy time and parent were confused in the disciplining of their children. The results of this is that parents were confused as to appropriate discipline for their own children. Read, "Tiger Mom" and do not take it out of contents. Her success is with her husband and children. Some parents are appalled by her techniques but her family is not and it was happening to them. We are cuddling our children and do not want to upset them. That is not good parenting. Remember consistence and discipline make for a secure child.

Children do not want their own way until you have made it a way of life or the norm in their life. An old habit then dies hard. It is hard to be out there on a limb making your own decision when it is not what everyone else is believing or doing. I applaud tiger mom.

If everyone is doing it, it must be ok or right. No, no, no.

A side note for me here is what are these children doing to their kidneys and bladder or other organs by being so engrossed in these games that they do not go to the bathroom and force their organs to be put on hold. That can be very costly in the long run. It is changing the way we view issues that will bring about the necessary changes in our culture. A paradigm shift takes place in order to make these necessary changes from one model for self or culture. Communication is the most essential part of a relationship so the first area to look at in your life for these changes to take place is, am I taking responsibility for what I say I want and talking about what I need. We should know what in our lives is not working for us anymore. Be creative and excited about change and not fear it. Be mindful that feelings lie to us and are not the true indicator for what is truth but is caused by your thinking. Again, thinking needs to be tweaked. What is the truth? Well, it is maybe best that we believe that there is none so that you will remain open to thinking, seeing and believing that everything is changing all the time. To be open and willing to allow for change in everything will help you discover more of truth but maybe not the full truth. Come as a little child, really meant to be open, curious, and creative. This is not discouraging but exciting. Einstein when he discovered the theory of relativity was applying it to a pacific application. When others took it step further, he really opposed them until it was proven in other applications. If you are like me, I use no receipt for some dishes, like chili or spaghetti and it never tastes the same but is always good to me. It is fun to use different applications and improvising is breaking the routine that can be boring. Your beliefs should not be stale but always open to a new twist. Is this not the reason we are in the mess we are now, because we did the same old thinking for years and did not apply new ideas to reflex the differences of today? Studying anything can bring new ideas to some old knowledge. Most of the time we are adding to old beliefs not erasing them. This knowledge can help in the fear of change, seeing that you are changing old beliefs because you now have new information, you are adding to your genetic by reprogramming them and future generations too. Your future generation, like all generations, have free will and may not want to go the path that you did or learn anything. I have eight siblings and none of them took my path. Our parents were very smart and wise. I asked the question of them that was different, so I had a different experience. Again, not right or wrong and good or bad. It just is. I realized that each of my siblings could have done the same as I did but chose their own path and because of free will. They all made more money that I did, so could be seen as more successful if you use that as a yardstick for success and culturally, we do.

Living in the real sense is getting excited about what we can learn by exploring new horizons and not staying content in our comfort zones. We are not highly evolved beings at all as we got stuck in materialism for too long. Success really needs to be defined more clearly. Rich and famous is where we focus and look at the results of that. Now rich and famous can be success if it is obtained fairly, advanced your soul, helped other and culture to advance. There are no favorites in heaven not even Jesus. The spirit of Jesus is doing the same thing in heaven that he did on earth, that is he is helping others to advance their soul because he was a very advanced soul. I believe he went into the wilderness and learned from all the wise elders as he wandered there between the age of 13 until we have an account of him in his 30's. The teachings of Jesus had all the flavor of all the old religions of his day as my writing here are from all the old teachings. There really is nothing new under the sun. It was created with the universe, so always was, and always will be.

We are just discovering what is. That is what makes me excited about the discoveries I make. I feel that I am just uncovering something that was there all the time and I had to do my part to be ready for the discovery. I am just getting a glimpse of what Jesus meant when he said, "Greater things you will do than this." We have regressed and limited ourselves. How? By not realizing what advancement are?

Let's take one of the most familiar one in healing. That was one of Jesus's greatest gift. Where is healing today? We depend on others and give our diseases up to others. I talk about this in the chapter on physical well-being but the power of thinking is primary here. You again are what you believe. Good news is that alternative techniques are again coming to the forefront. These ideas are not new but we are revisiting them and they do work as you will see that I have been using them and how they came about for me. My daughter did not want to be healed by my methods and she knew me well. I believe it was meant to be that way as the doctors she came in contact with were likely hearing her philosophy of life as the rest of us were. She taught on death and dying in her action more than words. Her master's thesis was to be on, "The meaning of life." She let me read the abstract and it was on target but it got to be a battle with a couple of her professor, who she though were her friends and it really did her in. She literally won the battle but lost the fight. After the department head oked her material she was so hurt she could not go on and then came the final cancer. I am not saying they were to blame as there is no blame, it is a good example of how we need to go inside and be of strong determination to override culture. One of the professors was Jewish and my daughter felt she had a hard time with the direction of the thesis. Our personal beliefs we operate from and this might be a good example. So we say we are followers of Jesus as Christians but few are really following as we give lip service and remain blind until we chose to do otherwise. That is really ok, stay there until it no longer serves you, as I certainly did. I really had a wonderful life but was not able to see it until I was ready. What took me so long was like everyone else as it is a lot of hard work to survive culturally and move ahead of culture at the same time. We feel the hard work as pain and struggle rather than seeing it as positive and growth. What is normal today is not normal for tomorrow. We want to be part of the group, so stepping outside the group is difficult and takes a good sense of self. If you are not strong enough in your personhood then you will fold back into the group. Being out there on the limb by yourself is being alone or at least feeling alone in your beliefs. Culture does not want you to be different for it will make them get out of their comfort zone. If you are not taking risks, you are not going anywhere so taking risks are important as not taking risks makes you at the mercy of the others. You will follow the sheep to slaughter.

The Bush administration used secrecy, broke constitutional rules and regulations at an alarming rate and will go down as the worst president in history or be recognized one day as the one who opened our eyes to what is wrong with our direction. We can at least conclude at this time that there seemed to be no one willing to stop the runaway train. The fear tactic were certainly know by those in power so now let's know these tactics and put the concepts to work in our own life.

There was a need for a Hitler and there was a need for a Bush. You have to get worst before you get better or move to a better place. What we do not learn from we are doomed to repeat. Where was democracy in all this? Wiretapping and labeling everything as anti-government certainly was enough to silence the people and most of us with little power were appalled by the lack of action or uprising. Side note here: ego was operating in any one that was in government at the time. See this or you miss the whole point of why we need to limit our government officials. Corruption comes in complacence. It was amazing how fast the US citizens lay down their rights in this case. Hitler took years to train his people to follow unopposed. I believe because I want too that Bush just took advantage of the twin towers incident but many still feel we ourselves had something to do with it. We did but only because we are not brotherly love and are adolescence.

Adolescence is selfish and want what they want and fail to see the consequences. How can foreign countries respect us? We talk the walk but not walk the talk.

Jesus did not war and could have saved himself as he knew what was in store for himself.

Maybe Bush was the messiah for too many. As the success of individual comes from within, the success or failure of the US will come from within. Jesus knew that the individual was the key to the group. We are only as good as our weakest link. So many of Jesus teachings were about the individual as that is all in the end that you are responsible for. It starts with one person and we are the key to the group. If you took pride in, I am not responsible and did not do anything. The did not do anything is the key. We are all one.

I am writing this book because, "To whom I give much, much is expected." I do not like that statement because of the burden it places on that should not be felt as a burden but at times it does. My voice in the wilderness says in response, "Who cares?" But I still write my letters to the editors and put myself out there in response to issues. My last letters were to five major newspapers about me and a friend's treatment when frisked at the airport after the full boding scanning was installed and I had refused to be full body scanned. "Why/" Read my chapter on physical well-being, it answers the why. Well maybe it did do good for that same airport this spring gave me a choice of security lines. Whew!

Again, in adolescence paranoia runs ramped. What do you have that you are afraid to give up or that someone wants it that badly?

Jesus came in the time of great need for change in the direction of the day, as all messiah's do. He really reminded us that all persons in the worlds are his children. I really see that Christians are killing my brother and sisters in the Muslin faith. Let's start there to change our beliefs. God does not have favorites or is not on one side or the others in wars. Pure love is all there is and you will become pure love in the end either in this life time or the many others. Stop separating yourself from others. "There but by the grace of God goes I." Get rid of ego.

The false self is in right-wrong and good-bad mode.

In spirit world there is no judgement there is observations so how does the soul want to advance? Well, it is like you being in the eighth grade and wanting to go to high school. You do not see it as right or wrong, just that it is the next step in your advancement. Your Being wants to advance because it no longer is being served by where it is. (This later you will see is like the many mansions in death you will not want to go where you do not fit in.) Comfort will be important in these cases.

When you follow your intuitions, it is not about outside indicators, it is about inside indicators. This is a glimpse of spirit operating. Ego is out of the way and the real self is coming thru. You are part of the tree of life or the Akaska Records. The more you use intuition the more it operates. If you override intuition, you usually fail and feel it and wish you had paid attention to it more. You did not because it was not the norm for you in trusting yourself, - after all who are you!!!

The more you honor intuition the more it increases. Practice, practice is the way with most new learning. Intuition is the true self, the higher self, the already knows, the essence of our Being, the spirit, the soul. Do not get caught up in man-made languages.

When I observe something, I am not making a judgement and it is important to know the difference. Observation is reporting what is and judgement is subjective. Judgement has a different feel to it like the feeling of right or wrong. That is the best I can do with it now.

When you start to rid yourself of ego, you are afraid of the new you and people around you will let you know that you are different and some will even not like the new you. The fear is ego in and of itself as we are familiar with our responses to circumstances. It feels like we do not care as much as before but you are actually care more in a different way and have dropped judgement. You are more objective. We are not responding from past experiences but we are in the NOW.

In psychology we call this process of letting go of our subjectiveness and being objective. Being objective takes the self out of the way and being judgmental. When you are out of the way then you see the situation, event, or person in a different way. You sort of see both sides of the coin. In my private practice, I can tell when I am out of the way, objective or ego and the true objective self is doing the therapy. It is awesome but it is not a conscious decision it is a way of Being. Here is another example: you have an experience and after feel really wonderful for you handled it well and are not sure of what you did, then ego was absent and true self was doing the Being. This I call, high on life and awesome. Bottle this and we would not need all those pills for everything. We would just Be and let everyone else Be. Go ahead and kill the body but you cannot kill the spirit.

Stress is another good aspect of getting rid of the ego, that is there is much less stress or no stress when you are not operating from ego and the past. Come as a little child, each experience is fresh, new, creative and approached with curiosity. You actually hear what is being said instead of projecting what is being said. You get rid of your programing and you operate in the NOW as little children do.

A friend of mine started drinking more after the death of a loved one. It scared her so she saute treatment for the drinking. She really was not feeling better but more depressed after seeing a male counselor for a while. She said she felt judged and depressed each time she left his office.

She wanted to know if that was normal or if she should seek other treatment. A superior attitude by counselor is not uncommon but not much help for the client, as pride can be a substitute for alcohol. I suggest that she deal with the grieving and loss more at this time. Cause and effect seemed to be the issue and not all alcoholism is the same. We all have an addiction of one sort or another as the culture has an addictive personality. Addiction is anything that is obsessed about and culturally we have a slew of them. I am not good enough, there is not enough money, not smart enough, not attractive, and where ever there is not enough it becomes an obsessive belief or behavior. Getting rid of our negative thoughts about ourselves and excepting what is, until we can change it is the place to start. Stress is usually in negative thoughts. Fears of not having enough or making mistakes. If focusing on the now, we can see that we have everything we need, then we clear our thoughts and find solutions to the issues. It really does require time alone to process where you are in your thinking of self.

A good point to ponder is, why do I let others tell me who I am? Since they are just assuming from their own experiences and may or may not be right. I am the only one that knows me. No one can know you as you are changing all the time either by choice or circumstances. In counseling I always hope I am giving options or choices but that the client has to conclude what will work for them and giving them several options it best. I can surmise what will happen if - but

I cannot know for sure. If I know for sure it will be ego and in spirit it will be mystery of the unknown for everyone is different. It really keeps me on my toes and I love that. The client maybe growing but so am I.

So if I am subjective I am ego and if I am objective I am spirit.

In the art of communication, the first point is to listen to hear and the second is clarification. It is necessary to clarify what is meant by what is being said and not assume you know. Webster says that listening is a chance to hear. I love that, it does not say we hear, which is a major part of the lack of understanding for we think we hear. That leads to clarification to really understand what someone else means by what is being said. When others assume they know what we mean by what we say then and do not ask for clarification then things really get misinterpreted or misunderstood. The only way to know what is meant is to ask. In groups I am asked sometimes what someone meant by what someone said and my response is I do not know. As I would have to ask for clarification too. I do not want to assume as it is a waste of energy. You do not know any more in assuming than you did before so do not assume, just know that you do not know.

Let go of ego who wants to know the answers to everything without asking what is meant. Language is the most misunderstood of forms of communication. So asking is necessary and get comfortable in asking for clarification.

If you are misunderstood in a communication, do not apologize for the receiver not getting it. If it left you with good intentions than keep it there and help the receiver to understand and get clarification. We would all become better communicators if we would do this. This is also a good place to start with validating yourself. You do not need to validate yourself out loud but just do it internally. If it left you as pure thought then it remains pure thought. That is validation of oneself.

It is good to examine if you take responsibility for self and others. If so, drop taking the blame or responsibility for others. We are all teachers as well as learners. Now teach others, if possible, to clarify. I use statement like, "Gee that is interesting that you took it that way. Or "That was not what I meant, why do you suppose you took it that way?" I think we fail to see how we are in this together and that in fact we each play a unique role in each other's growth and development. We are so afraid to offend that we fail each other. We are all therapists or teachers. Identify yourself as one. We will all experience the same things sooner or later. Been there done that. Our strong feelings about something usually have a connection in our life as it is in our DNA or genetics likely. Soul prints are saying the same thing. We live in the now which is greatly influenced by the past. Many unfounded fears are from the past lives. So it is good to know that when trying to work thru them. Some call it Karma. In fact, knowing so that you study, is a good way to work through them that seem to be reoccurring. Why know anything about past lives, you can do without knowing. Some persons are born with strong fears and de ju vi. Letting go frees up energy and focus. In the future it is likely we will be more open to all these concepts. It is like I do not believe in Saints but many do. No right or wrong, it is just where you are in your process. We are always advancing our beliefs and to me there are no favorites in spirit world as we know them in flesh world. It is harmful to me to have some persons raised to the level of being more than human as that is all they were. So many good people go unrewarded for the service they do with no position for reward. In fact, it is a talent that is a gift and needs no reward. If God has no favorite and that is a fleshly or earthy concept then it is for not. Rising above man-made concept is difficult but not impossible. Study other religions and cultures is very helpful. If I see action that contradicts beliefs then it is worth pondering. The growing you do is not a competition for anyone but self. That is all you are accountable for in the end.

We do need to be owners of our own behaviors. No one can make you do it! We say you made me do it when in fact it is not true, we are choosing to do it. I used to teach even if a gun is to your head, you have a choice and in fact you do. I did not say it was an easy choice but a choice none the less. If you see death and dying as not a bad choice than that could be considered a higher choice by many. You can kill the body but not the spirit is a higher concept.

There is no security in anything nor should there be. You are born, you die is the only security even if you have not processed death as a security yet. Once this is processed then it frees you to live free from the waste of energy spent on thinking about it. Know what you have control over and let go of the rest. Those that lost money to Bernie Madoff should know by now that he knew people very well and gave them what they wanted to hear. A good lesson in money and security, as both are illusions. FDIC protects your money, or does it? If the bank closes tomorrow, yes, your money is protected but how long do you think it will take for the money to be yours? How about three to four years and in the meantime what will you live on? Faults hope is not good planning.

Where did the pensions go, where are the moneys in the 401K's? Security there is none. So the point is look at what you believe is important and each time it should come down to family and friends. There is a life of everything, meaning organizations, cultures, countries, nations, and humans. Humans make up the all of all.

Everything has a life as systems do and always have. The tea party, I see breaking off from the Republican coat tails as it will not work attached to the old, as to many old timers will not change. I see limiting the office of government officials in everything to break special interests. I see us becoming more about community because mobile society made for loneliness. Our values will change from material to persons. What happens to one happens to all.

There is a good reason to embrace this idea and it is that the only thing that is important in the end is how you treated yourself and others including the animals and environment.

Unconditional love is the ultimate goal.

Physical Health

Since we were created not to be sick, then why are we? If the body was intended to heal itself then why do we not let it? If physicians were to heal themselves than why do we go to physicians?

I am asking you here not to give up your physician but to look at what was intended and how far from it we have strayed. There is a body mind connection to explore here. In Eastern medicine the whole being is treated. In Western we treat the disease and forget the body mind connection. It is getting better as the economics is dictating here as well as there seems to be no cure coming forth in many disorders then people are starting to not believe so much in our modern medicine. We do need to see the body mind connection and alternative beliefs. It is hard to change old belief and trust in self when for so long we have in Western turned our bodies over to so called authorities. Prevention is the key to good health.

Some forty years ago I took these questions seriously. I was experimenting with some biblical ideology. I had been reading the Bible cover to cover, which I have done five times, and studied it for about seventeen years. It is a very interesting book and you begin to see how we as humans have evolved with our thinking. So why are we now stuck in long ago as if God doesn't speak to us today. FEAR! The bible is a good history book as well as a good thinking book. My dedication got me moving ahead in thinking. God is dead was mouthed at this time about 1973, so boy did I feel like I was out there on the limb by myself. What doesn't kill you makes you stronger and I began to believe in myself. Even if you study the New Testament only, the teaching of Jesus is powerful and not about war. He however came to change what was not going in the right direction at that time. He stood up against the powerful of the day. That was his real purpose and change was much needed. He tried to move the times ahead and stop some of the corruption of the day. He was not conservative.

Well back to the physical health. If we were not intended to sick when created, then how do we get back to where we were meant to be? First, we need to believe that. Secondly, the desire to see it work or God says, "Test and try me". So I did. The first was leg cramp, while walking with my husband. When I petition God about the fact that I could not keep up with my husband if I was going to have leg cramps and we needed this time together, the cramps went away. Now this happened time and again. Whew!! Prayer is after all energy. And I was on my way to testing the healing of self and my need not to be sick. Now note that I wasn't really testing God but the need not to be sick, my body's need not to be sick. My body's ability to cure itself. The principle of sickness is being tested. God had already said that he did not create me to be sick. You do not test God for energy is it. I was balancing the energy in my leg by going to the pure energy source, God. I prefer to call God "Universal Mind" God did not name himself God so what works for you use it. Again, be willing to change is essential here too.

Now I have not been to a doctor in about forty years. I have blown out my knee, pulled a hamstring, sprained an ankle, shattered an elbow and mended them all by what I called at the time as energy transference. Now I might call it Reiki. I do not catch colds or have the flu. I take just Vit. C and glucosamine for my joints but have no arthritis as far as I know. I ski, both downhill and cross country, skate, golf, walk, snow blow and shovel, mow lawns all for the exercise. Exercise is very important and doing something that is fun as well as things that need to be done can be very rewarding. The holistic approach does not have to be boring.

When I was in Austria skiing in 1991, I blew out my knee and it swelled and would not stay in place. A physical therapist was in the group and she taught me what she called energy transference to get the swelling down. It was like magic as the pain went away when she or I put our hands on both sides of my knee. I was not going to miss a beat of the two-week trip and the accident happened the first day, so I walked everywhere on it. She said it would heal in thirteen weeks and it did. I went to New Zealand that July and had no problem. What puzzles me most about this is there is no damage and I walked on it every day. I am always in awe when these things happen.

This experience leads me onward toward learning about energy. I am a very curious person and love to learn or remember. I had a new concept to go into and attended seminars on magnetic energy and the use of magnets, which did not do much for me. But about this time, I was running into physic. All my reading was referring to the physics of energy. Now one definition of physics is the art of healing, of physics natural philosophy this seems to change the definition a little.

I was beginning to run into the marriage of physic and spirituality. These two fields of studies have always taken pride in the fact that they so not related but now they are coming together and overlapping. Exciting. I have always been seeking the truth, liberal in thinking and not comfortable in some of the old beliefs. They were just not ringing true for me anymore. Thinking out of the box is so necessary if we are to move ahead. In our country it is so not keeping the status quo that we need but new discoveries.

Fear has really kept us stuck in health and well-being issues. Fear keeps you looking to others for the answer to your well-being and like everything else it is inside. If you are to heal yourself it is to you, you have to rely. Have you heard that you bring to you what you fear? The law of attraction it is called at times. Well, you can and do if you do not work on the fear to disspell it. I have a 93-year-old male friend that I have tried to get him to see that he was programming himself to be sick. He is beginning to see it. As every time someone coughed around him, he would cover his nose and mouth, telling himself that he was going to get their cold. I got him to stop reacting and just let whatever happened to be. It is that simple. Nothing to fear but fear itself and there is no death lest you make it so. Get in there and work on these two concepts and change your beliefs.

In Ayurvedia medicine theory; disease or sickness comes as a result of an individual's forgetfulness of its internal or divine map. I love that, it is beautiful. Go inside and remember who you are and who you want to be. The messages that you give yourself should be, I want to be healthy. Then you remember it until every cell in your body knows that you know it to be true, that we were not intended to be sick. Dis-ease - get rid of the dis and fear and be at ease. Is not that what my 93-year-old had to learn? Be at ease do not take on the disease. Once you get the technique of changing the way you think of things, you will use it every day and it will become second nature to you.

Remember when you got busy, your headache went away? Focusing away from the pains will take away their power and until you focus again on it there can be relief. Over worked muscles, leg cramps, colds and other non-threatening ailment went away for me. At that time in my life prayer as a distraction from letting my mind focus on them was the technique I used. Now prayer is energy. It was exciting and magic for me. I felt that I was being taught or remembering that I did not have to let this be in my body. I was in my 30's at this time. Today I know that my consciousness knows that I know as every cell in my body knows that I was not meant to be with sickness or ailment. I have however been very hard on my body as I am always very physical, ice skating, roller skating, water skiing, golfing; golfing sometimes four times a week for walking 18 holes, downhill skiing as well as cross country and at 62 learned to scuba dive and have over 17 open dives. My point is that I have over worked my joint but as far as I

know I have no arthritis and I still use energy transference or Reiki to heal since I have had other injuries.

Injuries usually happen when you are stressed and overtired, so it is cause and effect as the consequences for fatigue. No one is doing this to you as we like to blame God or someone else and that is a waste of energy, for we do it to ourselves or bring it to us as again in the law of attraction.

How do you answer the law of attraction? Change the way you think and then you will not bring this to you anymore. This is the answer to another important mystery as for years something may have been in your face as an irritant and as soon as you change the way you responded to it, it went away. Now it did not go away as much as it was no longer a focus for you. We would sometimes marvel at its disappearance and say did it change or did I change? But it is always the one that is irritated that changed as there is no reason for the others to change unless they want to.

I believe I have healing hands but my daughter knew of my beliefs in self-healing and yet she wanted no part of it. That was a hard lesson for me. I believe it was not part of her journey this time and she knew it. Her purpose and understanding in this time around was what she taught the rest of us especially me in death and dying and the essence of life. She used to tease me about reincarnation when I wanted to get to that later. She used to think it was silly that everyone did not believe in it. One life to get it right was laughable. She wrote a book of 800 pages about one of her past lives. She wrote it in about eight months and the details in the book were so vivid you knew she had to live it to write with such knowledge. Her knowledge in the book was more than she had lived this time around. When I asked her how she knew something in the book, she would just give me that laugh of; Mom you are not getting it yet. But when I said this is a past life isn't it, she said, "yes". The book never got published and that is ok. She studied philosophy for eleven years in college as there she was at home in her own world. We had many philosophical discussions as at the same time I was feeling very alone in my own learning. Healing is not meant to be for all.

Again, we are body, mind and spirit. The body needs food and nutrition, exercise and cleanliness.

The mind need exercise through challenges and stimulation. The spirit needs awareness to increase and remember spirit is not religion, it is the essence of you or your potential. Growth and development is what the spirit really thrives on. There is a guarantee that if you are experiencing all these aspects then you will be happy. Now happiness is contentment and peace of mind. It is not a guarantee that you will not have trials and tribulations. For they are growth producing. Materialism will not make you happy for very long. You get one goal accomplished and it is short lived as happiness. Lasting happiness is awareness. Awareness of what? Awareness is defined as having perception or knowledge (a consciousness) and informed. It is not material so it must be of the body, mind and spirit. The body is important but likely the least important as it dies and does not have eternal life. It does however support the mind and spirit while we are human. So it needs care to be healthy.

Yesterday I crossed country skied. I felt so good with the exercise. My message to myself when I do the exercising is that the body is important as a temple of the spirit and mind. I do not say that the body houses the spirit as the spirit is in the body and also around the body as it is energy.

The mind and spirit are not really separate as the spirit is more than the mind in the level of awareness. This is at the conscious level. A little fuzzy here if you cannot see the awareness of one over the other. All you need is inside you. You are aware of a small portion of what is in there or at the conscious level. Subconscious does know a lot you are not aware of. It is predicted that in the 21st century we will become more aware of much. In psychology we call the mind: the conscious and subconscious and it is all energy, so where does one start and the other leave off. I say, "I know this or that". I am referring to the conscious mind. Now what is subconscious mind?

It is spirit or the all-knowing. The spirit is trying to get you to become aware. You are in charge of what you want in this life time to become aware of. I laugh here as I wanted to know everything. My curiosity really did kill the cat, almost. My Mom was right to tell me not to learn it and I would not have to do it. I never listened and went right ahead and gathered all the experiences I could. It has been a good life.

It is said that 95% of our dis-eases are stress related, so the need to reduce stress in our lives is important and necessary today. Events may not change but the way we respond to them must.

It is the thinking that needs to change. Stressless is being at ease not that bad thing does not happen to good people. So if you are with dis-ease take a look at your stressor's. Fear of change is prevalent in our culture. It is said that 25 million Americans have panic attacks. "Why?"

Since the root of this is fear, where is it coming from? I lead a panic disorder group for nine year and most of the clients were Catholic. They discovered this I did not. It is a fear-based religion.

God was definitely conditional love. God was just condemning everything and Protestant went to hell when I grew up. Now it is difficult to move out of this type of fears when it was seemingly coming from the authorities of the day. Seeing God as unconditional love is needed to replace the fears of never being good enough. God does not make junk and you are a very important unique individual. Move to that belief of your self will be the truth and free you to be you. Take back your power and do not give it others. Spirit comes to earth in us to experience itself or God through our experiences. We are here to advance our soul. It is hard to advance your soul in negative energy. So God has to love me regardless of what I do. He cannot hate what he created.

Fears play havoc with the physical body. Feeling loved is what we all seek and is as close as yourself. You must love yourself before you can love others. God is all loving: the omni of love.

Omni means all present in everything.

So spirit or God experiences everything we do, as we are all one. Energy is in everything, around everything and is everything. This is not an easy concept but when we get it everything takes on a different light and we behave differently towards it, whether it is plants, people, trees or animals.

Everything is spirit or energy. Fire might be thought of as the common denominator since it all can burn and give off energy. So everything is spirit, energy and God. This is how we are all one at least one aspect of the oneness. You are an individual, you are a part and you are the whole.

When you come right down to it; we are all more alike than different. When something goes wrong; we separate from it and say, "I cannot understand how someone can do that?" That means that you do not understand self. As we are all capable of the same behaviors but we may choose not to do that. Do you ever hear the media act as if they cannot understand the behavior of others? Are you capable of anger? Yes! Everyone is. We do not look for cause but look for blame. Blame keeps us dead in the water, we must go beyond blame to cause. I believe we use statement like, "how could they," because we do not want to look at culture and what is wrong with it. If you say, you cannot understand, you will not understand. The thought stops there, with no real learning going on. You are what you believe." There but by the grace of God goes I" maybe a good statement at this time. Your flesh is weak at times and is just as capable of everything that any other human is but choices make the different. Culture wise we all play a part in the all either by being involved or the lack of involvement.

Stress again is the cause of most disorders, so the reduction of stress is really learning to see and think things differently. A good sense of self does not eliminate the flaws, it looks at how to change behaviors by changing how we look at them. Most stressors are cause by anger or fears.

Getting to the root of the anger and fears will reduce the stressor's and eliminate disorders. The body has just so many ways of responding to the stress and usually it comes out in breaking down the immune system, therefore producing disorders or diseases.

Techniques for Reducing Stress

The first techniques is still changing your thinking but next it helps to do some relaxation techniques as all of us will still have trial and tribulations in life. Meditation is easy to learn and very important in reducing stress, anxiety and panic attacks. I will give you some easy steps here but if you want more, take a class in yoga or spirituality. None of these are new techniques as they have been around since the beginning of time. They were used more in Hinduism, and Buddhism but again Jesus went of the garden to meditate. Time alone is the real concept and there is no right or wrong to it. Buddhism is not a religion but a way of life. So we might say it is important to put meditation or centering down or being alone as a necessary way of life. Teach your children on a warm summer day to lay down in the yard and gaze at the stars and ponder life there. The vastness of it all is an analogy of life. These techniques vary in so many ways you could not count them so there is no right or wrong way. Add and subtract anything that feels right for you. At first you will say, you felt no different and that is normal.

We have four brain waves; alpha, beta, delta, and theta. If you are reading this you are in beta and the alpha brain wave is that mellow feeling you get just before you go to sleep. If someone calls your name or the phone ring, you may hear it but do not want to respond. It is a really good feeling. Everyone who can fall asleep can be in this alpha state. You can fall asleep or you can choose to be super consciously alert or selectively alert that is alpha or hypnotic stage.

Now get in a place where you will not be disturbed and it is quiet. Make sure your clothes are loose and comfortable. Laying position is best at first and later any position will do. Now making a simple tape of these instructions can help you listen and follow. Soft music as a background is good if you make a tape and of course a minute or so pause is necessary between each deep breathe and visualization.

So let's get to the alpha state.

Now I want you to lay (sit) flat with your arms by your side with palms up. Close your eyes and take a deep breathe and hold it for three seconds and then release it. Now do this three times and then let your breathing slow to normal. Breathing should be from the diaphragm which says that the tummy moves in and out not the chest.

Now visualize with your mind's eye, which is in the brow just above the nose, that you are in your favorite place in the universe, it might be a garden, a beach, a park, a room or outer space. Put all the ingredients needed to make it yours and special. No right or wrong.

Lay down or the equivalence of laying down in your special spot. Get comfortable by starting at your top of your head and with your mind's eye sense your relaxing the top of your head by taking a deep breathe, after a minute go to your forehead and relax it. After a half minute go to your eyes, now if the eyes want to be a creak open let them do not force them closed, relax them. Now go to the ears, shut out all sounds but those of the tape or the special sounds in your special place.

(This is selective hearing technique). Now go to your cheek muscles and relax them by taking a deep breathe. Go to your nose and hear the sound of your breathing. In and out - In and out Relax.

Come down to your mouth and relax it by breathing in and out. Visualize your neck now and relax it. This is the most important part of the body in relaxation as all the blood that goes to the brain flow thru the neck carrying important oxygen to the brain. (Neck exercises are very important aside from relaxation.) Take a deep breathe and let those shoulders relax. Neck and shoulders relax together.

Feel the deep relaxation in the shoulders and neck for a minute.

Now go to the arms, wrists and hands. Feel all the tension go out the finger tips and relax.

Take a deep breathe and go to the chest and relax it. Feel the heart beating and sense the heart chakra opening up to let the energy flow through. Sense the seat of love and life here. Love yourself at this level.

Let's go to the waist at the navel and relax it. This chakra is the solar plexus, the seat of emotions, balance and brotherhood.

Next to the tummy, the seat of the soul and relax by taking a deep breathe. Visualize the freedom of Being here as you let go of the negative and move into the positive light.

The first or last chakra is the root or base. It is located at the base of the spine. Here is that which represents the nature of things or being grounded. Take a deep breathe and relax.

Come down your hips and relax them. Then your knees, calves, and to your feet and feel all the tension go out your toes.

Then take an assessment of your whole body and any area that is still tense focus on it and let go of any tension there.

That is all there is to relaxation of the body. Once it is done you can focus again on your special place and accomplish whatever you want. It maybe just to relax and let go of the day or it maybe to stop a behavior and change your thinking. It can be to receive a revelation. You can imagine your life and what it is you want it to be. Do this visualization and then just bring yourself back to your real place. Some use the count of three to return to your room. You should feel more confident and relaxed. Remember you came to this world with lots of dreams and aspirations now make them come true.

Being sure of what you want is really important for many times we are not sure. The universe cannot bring you the desires of your heart if you are not sure or ready.

Other techniques to reduce stress are exercise, music, gardening, sports, being with others, and any passion that helps you let go of the stressor and focus away to a more positive place.

Death and Dying

After years of running a panic disorder group several issues seemed to surface within the disorder. Panic disorder is about extreme unfounded fears. It was said that 25million US citizens were subject to these kinds of fears. In group we explored cause and effect and found several common belief systems that were common with each group members. The greatest of fears would be death and dying, not necessary that we would die but how we would die. Which lead us to control issues. Which lead to expectation. Which lead us to beliefs.

Einstein stated that "everything is energy or it is nothing. "We are spiritual beings having an human experience. We are all one. Life is different when you believe this. Everything changes once you understand the spirit or energy of everything. To me it makes sense. Like the air in this room, you do not know where it begins or ends. Or you do not know where the wind comes from or where it goes. Yes, I can say it comes from the East or West but where is it's beginning or end. It likely does not have one.

I cannot believe in WAR or killing as it just does not make sense to me. Because I know you can kill the body but not the spirit and I or my true self is Spirit. I am not the body as the I AM is Spirit. So if we knew this as a culture everything would change. We would see things so differently, like death. Where is thy sting oh death? Death is positive so fear not.

A positive attitude toward death will not make us more apt to be destructive but more responsible. I take or try to take better care of my body, mind and spirit with a positive outlook toward death.

Dichotomy:

Love my body but at the same time wanting to be free of my body. It is not about death and dying as much as about going home. We are again spiritual beings having a human experience. My spirit is all around and through me, my body is heavy and incases my organs that keep me alive. Spirit is light energy This may at times seem like suicide but it is not at all. It is the beauty or positiveness in death. A longing for HOME. Death is positive if birth is positive. The inevitable is that we are moving toward death the minute we a born. If you do not get to this belief than death hangs over your head and is a negative. If negative than it is not true and why believe an untruth. The truth sets you free. Move toward the light…no punt meant!!! This will cut loose any anxiety around death and dying and other issues in our life. Power and control are big issues with those who see death as negative. Fear is still the driving force. And that leaves you vulnerable to the direction of others. Fear has been a tool used by others for power and control over others. Fear is useless except to help you grow and learn by conquering whatever it is that you fear. Do not avoid it but see what is waiting for you in the change and the change will be in the thinking not the environment. Replace fears with new beliefs. Let's take death; God was the first thing that comes to mind and how he is going to judge you. Well, that does not happen. God is spirit and spirit is energy as you are, you and God are one. You and I are one as we are spirit and it is hard to tell where you begin and end and where I begin and end in spirit. Got it yet? God is in everything and so is spirit. Energy remains constant so in death you still are. My awareness has increased toward all body, mind and spirit aspects. Awareness or enlightenment comes to the forefront now, I see with new eyes. It really gives you freedom and control.

Why have we not advanced very far in this culture? The biggest issue has been, like death and dying, fears; FEAR has been used for control and power over others. That is not love for we should not want power and control over others.

I am a psychotherapist and I see my first responsibility to others is to equip them with tools to empower them in their life. To keep these tools for myself and not share them is just selfishness.

Are we a selfish culture? Yes. We are adolescence at our best. Adolescence is about the self. It is not right or wrong as you need to pass through that phase in order to go to the next phase, young adulthood.

It would not be incorrect to state that we are very primitive in our thinking. We are not aware of how powerful thinking is. It is energy; put enough energy together and that is bomb force. So if thinking is energy and we all thought alike whatever we were thinking would come into view. Whew!!!

What a powerhouse! Just in thinking. So we can think ourselves to a better place if enough of us want the same thing to happen. Look at the walls of Jericho - believing and sound brought the walls down and the walls fell inward and not on the believers. They have uncovered ruins that prove the walls fell inward. Neat!!

What is prayer? It is thinking. Why do people who are being prayed for say that they felt the prayers? The energy pushed against them. Neat!! Since we are all energy, we can say the energy joined their energy.

So think, think, think. Now there is a dichotomy here because in mediation you clear your mind of ruminating thoughts. There are times for both. We meditate to center down and clear the mind to hear that still small voice. Now thinking as in pondering is the kind of thoughts that bring revelations and are growth producing. Letting go of something you cannot change is the thinking that mediation sets aside. You do not have to sit or lay down to mediate Some can be done while you do routine things such as dishes, vacuuming, or one I liked is long drives. It is really like self-hypnosis and I know that it is said to not do this while driving but I find I am more alert but know yourself before trying it. It was a blessing when I

would travel alone for six or seven hours. We are all unique and that is the dichotomy as there are no concrete rules for thinking.

This takes me to another idea - if you do not come to the same conclusion on a topic, do not think that you are wrong and someone else is right. There is no wrong or right!! Each individual is different enough and at a different place in life to conclude differently and both can be right -if right should be used here. We spend too much time looking outside ourselves when our answer for us is inside. All that you need is inside. The Bible even states this over and over everything you need is inside. It says," there are rivers, wells and all there is to remember inside," so go inside for your truth. Our experiences are our teachers and our experiences are different enough to conclude differently. If in our experiences we could find the positive all suffering would disappear. We get stuck in the feelings instead of using pain as the motivator to think and grow We will grow if we ask it," what is it trying to teach us. What can I learn from this experience?" Have the experience and do not try to push it away. Learn from it so you can move on and you will not have to experience it over and over. Go inside and think for yourself. Our culture is negative so no help there. Ever tell someone you are going to do something and they do not agree that you should do it? What they are really saying is, "I could not do that". They are no help but that does not mean that it is not for you.

We are reprogramming our old pathways or neurons in the brain when we change the way we think. Old habits die hard. So it will take practice, practice, practice. But the old belief will be replaced by the new beliefs. Why do we fight with ourselves at this time? We really have a lot of doubt of whether we are right in giving up old beliefs. It is natural part of the process. This feels like guilt and it is a choice, so practice and the feelings will change and you will learn not to stay in the feelings for long the next time. Read, "I'm OK, You're OK" from the 70's.

You are what you believe and you will act on that belief. ACT on what you believe therefore affect your behavior and feelings. So if I do not like my feelings I go back to what am I thinking and if I do not like my behavior I go back to what am I thinking as it all goes back to beliefs and thinking. We need a paradigm shift in our thinking and fears keep us afraid to do the changing or shifting of old beliefs. The greatest fears are connected to God given to us likely by the church. Churches have not moved from the dark ages but if you see them as a foundation and move beyond the foundation than a shift will come in thinking. You are not giving up your old beliefs as much adding or expounding upon them. You are not giving up the foundation, you are building on it.

Normal is just what the majority believe today, it does not make it so. Here is one belief that really gets me! To say you are conservative is to be stuck, our government is using that for the majority as they are stuck and they know it. It is used for all those Christians to manipulate them and get votes. Ignorance is bliss It is saying you have a big fear of change or thinking out of the box and in our tough times right now, reinventing the wheel is not going to cut it. Creativity is needed and the entrepreneur is needed. One who will take risks and is not conservative. Let it be you and do not run on the coat tails of others. If the old is not working and got us to where we are, why would you want to keep trying it. This is the same analogy that it takes to change your thinking, a paradigm shift. Conservatives fear moving ahead in thinking. Your government is not at all conservative, it just uses the word to get the stuck majority on board. Be aware of those in sheep's clothing. We will have to limit the terms of our government in order for them to do the right thing as most of the old senators and representatives are just furthering their careers and not for the people. It really is all about the fear of change. The good news today is that many are getting this. If we had gone willingly for change, we would not be in this position now and now you can see why we learn from our mistakes or disaster and not before. George W. Bush used fear tactics to shut the US citizens up with his use of wiretapping and secrecy. We let him abuse the power of the government and ignore the constitution. How lame is that? The real fallout from this abuse is yet to come. So if you think it's bad now, wait. The worst will be when we bring our troops home and no finances to support them and their families. Why are we taking advantage of the unrest in Egypt, Libya and the countries to follow. The US has no money so it gives our government the right to borrow for war. Sad!! Of course, hind sight is always fifty- fifty so you can see getting into the war was all wrong in the first place. But who was going to oppose the President after 9/11. Good move, No! Take a good look at Egypt and etc. as that will be us soon.

Christianity has really gone amuck. We are not Christ like at all. Jesus was an anointed Christ.

Christ meaning a savior. Most US citizens do not know the difference and that maybe the issue. More on that later.

So you are what you think or believe. Change the thinking on death and dying and come to the conclusion that you really never die, that you have eternal life and you can just take a new form upon the death of the body. In doing so you will live now free of the fear of death and dying. You would in this belief, then see everything differently. You would see that we are all one in the world and what happens to one is happening to all. Take the present economy it is affecting the world and seemed to start with the US. We do depend on each other but do not act it yet. Every new law affects you, every new tax affects you and etc. I would rather crash now than later. Are we not just delaying the inevitable?

Let's go back to the death and dying issues? What are the fears? How we die is one of them. Here is the real reasoning for there is nothing to fear but fear itself. True you will not know how or when (to a point) that you will die, but it really should not matter. Why, because the body will sustain just so much pain then it will shut down. The soul, knowing this will leave the body if it hasn't already. I am not the body. I am the spiritual being. You are likely already hovering over your body and do not feel any pain and your knowing goes with the spirit when you die. The knowing survives with the spirit. Life is eternal. The spirit is not emotional. It only experiences joy, love, acceptance, peace or other positive attributes. Knowing this will help you leave your body. It is really an out of body experience if you have not remembered one before as your soul leaves your body in sleep likely every night to be replenished or regenerated as we can be slow to grow and the spirit gets bored with us, is one way to look at it.

So fear not how you will die as it is likely taken care of in our creation of being. You are an important unique individual and loved enough to be spared in death. My father died at 57, as he had farm related asthma. On the way to the hospital for a routine fluid reduction he was telling my Mother, how to dispose of the farm equipment and etc. He knew he was not going to return with her. She was very amazed but it was also very consoling as she knew there was more to life than meets the eye. My Mom was a very wise person so it was more added proof about life and death. She was 88 when she died and a year before she did, she told me she was ready to go home.

Home was her word and we should be more aware of when it is time to move on to spirit world.

Next fear! What is waiting for us on the other side?

Life is eternal. Let's dissect that idea. We have witnessed the body dying so it is not the body, so what else is there? It is the essence of you, which is the soul including the mind. Some of the other names we give soul are spirit, aura, energy, or ether. Now the mind, which is in every cell in your body not just the brain of the individual goes with the spirit and is part of the spirit. Every cell in your body has a mind of its own. So this is a good reason to work on your thinking. Do not take with you stinking thinking… Cells are programmed with energy. My liver cell is not my blood cell. We have a new body every seven years. The main substance is energy and thinking is energy. Whew!

So, our energy is not separate from the spirit as all is connected as energy is free flowing with no beginning or ending in a sense unless restricted in some way like in a bottle, bomb and etc. Now it is easier to see how it is eternal.

Next question might be, ok what is my spirit or soul doing?

Your soul is trying to advance your awareness. The soul already knows but finds it freedom when you know. Remember it is trapped in your body and does not go against your knowing at least until you are ready to receive. Since part of you already knows, your soul is trying to get your consciousness to know or be aware. Keep in mind this is all energy. How? Your dreams, experiences, situations, or events. There are no coincidences, luck. or such but learning growing experiences. When something happens try to learn from it and what you learn practice until it becomes a part of your awareness. We can have head knowledge and it still not be what I call heart knowledge. That it is not yet part of our being. Example is calling yourself a Christian and not acting Christian. You are trying to be that is good, but Jesus showed the way. Now follow his examples. War is not one of his examples. It is not just important to know something in the mind, it must be practiced to be really known. Practice, practice and it will become part of you so to speak. Then you can put into practice what you know. If I'm love, I can't be showing hate. Again, the most obvious example is our calling ourselves Christian and not acting like a savior but very destructive. Jesus and the father are one because they are both unconditional love. Jesus was a Christ or a savior of Christians. To be Christ like is to be a highly evolved being. We should announce that we are becoming Christ like. "I am" announces that I have arrived at being something. "I am that I am". I am in the making. I am evolving. So we have to practice what we know for it to become part of our being. Now so to speak you own that thinking, behavior or feeling.

If we are to move from being an adolescence culture, we need to process in honesty where we are and where we want to go and be more responsible for our behavior. We think it is ok or justified when there is no good excuse. If you want to know what is wrong with our culture in the US, just ask a 17-year-old or even younger. They say it like it is and are right on target. We could use them as a mirror to see our culture. I love it, no lost generation here. They say, "look who's running the show? "And then say, "they do not know what to do about the mess." Some resign to rebelling as it does not make sense to them. We are all responsible for what they do. Yes, until you get to believe this, you are dead in the water. You cannot grow until you start to take responsibility for self and how we affect others. Culturally we point fingers but do not want to look at our contribution to the problem. We are all one and what affects one of us affects us all. Yes, you can take anything and turn it into positive or negative. Why not choose positive. We are a negative culture that seems to thrive on violence and horror. Take these writings. You can say, it is negative, because I say we are not in a good place! Or you can say it is positive as I am trying to teach us how to get to a higher place. It is all in where you want to go. Most seem to want nothing to change, they are conservative and yes, I am liberal and want to move ahead, not so much for my sake, but culturally before we self-destruct.

Can not you see the US has likely already run its course. All nations of the world have had their time in history; the fall of empires like Egypt, Rome, England, Spain, France, Germany, Russia, Austria/Hungary, China and etc. Do we really learn from history or are doomed to repeat it? Now look at the nations that are on the horizon; India, Africa, and South America. They are rich in resources and maybe that is the plan, for as the focus shifts away from us, we will have time to grow up. As the stage from adolescence to community usually takes a time to be set apart. A time to let go of the past and focus on the Now. Now, not even the future for it is so unknown or unpredictable. Are we there now!! Almost!! The crash is still to come for those who have not felt the sting. It rains equally on the rich and the poor. We have free will and can change but as history really proves that we do not until we are forced too. The haves do not share with the haves not as they could. Sad but true. Try to at least be aware and change self as that is the only one, we have control or power over in the end. Is that not a nice picture of our illusions? We think we have power over others but it is all an illusion. Start with your illusions so that change in you can take place.

Remember the song, "Free to be Me"? Well, that is our quest and that is freedom, each time we expound on our illusions we move closer to that freedom that we so quest for. So the soul is trying to advance our awareness. Giving you back to yourself. The real self. In psychology we might say that the subconscious is trying to make the conscious aware. In death the soul leaves the body and it does leave the body while you sleep also. You really give permission to die. We seem to know when it is time to leave planet earth especially if we have had a good life and are not hanging onto life for self or others. There are some who die and were not ready so they hang around in their place of death. This is a good reason to process your view of death and dying while living on planet earth. You will not know everything to expect but may have a comfort zone in it all. Culturally we have had our heads in the sand about what to expect and I believe it was either because the supposedly experts did not know or they did not want you to know for power and control over the masses. The point is that if you have had a conscious life then you will know when to leave and some what to expect. You will at least feel good about it and that alone will be helpful in death. You can know your purpose on earth this time around if you will connect the dots of your life.

I have always been a psychotherapist and philosopher. I did not always know that or even want that. But at this stage of connecting the dots of my life I can see the Being. If you say or you hear someone, say I am just a housewife, doctor, mailman or such, then they are saying they do not see it as a viable service or purpose. Loving what you do takes realizing it is a value, therefore giving you value. Some are afraid to love what they do as they likely have not processed a healthy feeling toward themselves. Culture has taught them that they are not important. This is a good place to start to process your view of self and check out if you tell yourself, you are lovable and important. Everyone is! Hurt and pain have kept us from seeing this. Most religions have taught us that it is about others and not self, when it really is all about self. A happy person has much to give away, so getting happy comes first. It is not really about doing it is about being. It is true that the being will take care of the doing. Doing the right thing for the right reasons is pure happiness. Doing for the sake of doing for ego is just not fulfilling for long.

Dealing with the issues frees you to live, really live.

Where does the soul go when you die? We have not been taught much in this area by our religions Some religions have done better than others. First there is only heaven; there is no hell lest you make there one. Shakespeare said that years ago. Why did we not pay attention to that?

Until now with the New Age concepts being very vocal and prolific writers, the church rained or was thought to be the authority on these issues. The churches have labelled the new age stuff as negative but it does not seem to have the power over that it once did. Churches are in the dark ages and would like us to stay there. Fear and damnation are passay and the younger generations are not buying God as a negative but as unconditional love. Out of the mouth of babes. Thinking out of the box is the only way to growth. You have to realize that there is something missing when you know God-Spirit as love and you do not see love being spoken or in action. Our institutions are just made up of ordinary people. The fall of the Catholic church from grace really open eyes.

I knew I had baggage so I knew institutions had baggage. As I read the Bible cover to cover almost five times and studied it for 17 years it began to tell me a different story each time. As I grew, I saw it as a history recorder and a thinking process. As thinking changed as history changed. Neat!!

Another change for me was the metaphysics in it all. I started to feel alone in my experiences with the spirit and metaphysics. There seemed to be no one to relate in it all, yet there it was in the bible. I had at this time an out of body experience and my life passed before for no apparent reason. I was not in any parallel. I was also teaching a six grade Sunday school class when a couple of the students started to tell me of a seance they took part in, in the church kitchen and a body was produced. It was true I was told later. About this time, I had an experience as a vision, as there was 10 acres of wood lot next to our home and a fire was set twice, once when we were not home and the neighbors put it out and once when we were there. The paper boy came to collect one day and I saw him in flames and confronted him about the fires, telling him that he would not set any more and he agreed that he would not.

I attended the church I grew up in, the Methodist Church as well as a Pentecostal church and was experiencing the spirit world more. Some 5 years earlier I had what is said to be a born-again experience which I now call a first principles passion. It is a passion for following the principles of Christ. It is a way of life. In the Pentecostal church I was experiencing the teachings of the spirit and one of the teachings was that all of us have a gift of the spirit. Mine turned out to be prophesy and it was not the one I wanted, after all they killed the prophets. I really got angry with God over this one but did not know any better. Well, I did do one thing and that was to learn what prophesy entailed. Smart move. It is not just negative foretelling, I learned but also insightful revelations. What should psychotherapy really be? I also believe that we are all at times open to being spoke persons in revelations if we are open. The experience was a good teacher for me in how patience the universe is with us and will not force on us anything that we are not ready for. Now I have not been stoned yet??

I want to take the time here to talk about the still small voice that we are to be quiet and listen for.

For the most part it is within that it is usually heard. It likely should not be called a voice at all but because it is energy, it should be called telepathy. Telepathy is defined as apparent communication from one mind to another otherwise than through known sensory channels.

Remember, not known today may be known tomorrow for some. I love sensory channels as how do we describe our contact in sensory but with energy. Feel, touch, smell, hear, and see all energy or sensory. "My sheep will know my voice". My experience has always been that it is gentle, smooth and calming. It has never been harsh or angry, however in humor it is firm. If I question the voice and I do, then the voice changes not and just repeat the statement again. I am a doubting Thomas and question everything, but a sense of humor is always there. It is so awesome that I cry much of the time after an encounter with the experience.

Even as a small child why was always on my lips. My parents seemed to be very patient with me and my Mom was a very wise person. I guess I was a philosopher at a very young age. I had a strong drive to learn and know. Mom would say," Lois if you don't learn to do it you will not have to do it". Never understood why she said that but it turned out to be true. To whom I give much is expected. My parents seem to have the right answer for me and they left me with some gentle traits. So my questioning comes naturally and a sense of humor is needed to put up with it.

Did you ever read the little book, "God it's Me Margaret"? Well, I just say, "It's me Lois, so get your humor hat on God". This was in the 70's so I

already knew that God, Spirit, Energy had a sense of humor. All of my past has been preparing me for a personal relationship with spirit, that is unique but for all. There were never any short cuts to knowing as reading and studying were necessary to get to think out of the box and my questioning a very important ingredient in it all.

If you do not question what you already know or what you are being taught then you miss what is for you. Everyone does not have the same experience the same way as we are very unique. We are unique, important individuals. I came from one of nine children and none of us had the same experiences with our parents. Not wrong or right-good or bad; just was. We are close in many ways and look out for one another as big families usually do. We come by laughter naturally and a sense of humor. We come together seven to ten times a year. Food is terrific and laughter is abounded. We may not have solved the world's problems but we lifted everyone spirit.

To answer further where the spirit goes when you die, is as varied as much as there is individuals.

In other words, we are unique enough to be at different stages of growth and development and our experiences get acknowledged that differently also. There is no better or worse place that you will experience unless you have created it. And it is best to change that concept before you die. You maybe confused at first but there will be loving spirits there to help you. These spirits are either loved ones that have already crossed over or people spirits that are aware of what you need to process your death. Life is what you make it and in death is what you make it except that there is no hell, lest you make it so. So start clearing your mind of a hell. It is that simple.

I was always seeking the truth, that is why all the questions even as a little girl. Even when raising my children, I read everything on parenting. I stayed home for nineteen years to raise them and was going to be the best possible parent I could be. I never thought I knew it all, I knew I needed to learn it. I was in awe, when the day before I needed to know an answer for my children it was there just in time. I also got direction from my children that was awesome. I really believe they taught me more than I taught them, if we just pay attention.

You do get what you need. One day, my boys were playing outside the kitchen window with friends and they had decided to go to a friend's home. My son said he would be right back, he was going to tell his mother where he was going. The friend said, "why do you always tell your mother?" My son replied that if my mom needs to find me in an emergency she will know where to start looking. I am a very sensitive person, so tears weld up and I am sure he got a hug when he came in.

You will get confirmation when you need it and you need to see the need to learn. Reading is my way of learning or rather my confirmation, however that again is not everyone's. We are all different. I first learn it in my head and then read for knowing I am on the right track. I am a doubting Thomas.

Now all of this processing will help you to know where to go when you die and you will feel comfortable in it if it is foreseen. Why be blind? There are many mansions and you will go where you are comfortable. It will be where your Being senses the comfort without question. You will not sense anything but belonging. No right or wrong or higher or lower, those are earthly concepts. Belonging is unconditional love. You will not go where you do not want to go or where you do not know. Your beliefs go with you in spirit and so it is important that you have an idea of what you want to experience. I have announced that I want to go to the bottom of the oceans as I am a scuba diver and love the mystery of the oceans. Maybe a little far-fetched. Let me give you an example of what I think. A one-year-old dies, no problem for them as they just left spirit world, so they have not forgotten it yet and go right back where they came from. They likely did not come to planet earth for their sake but someone else, the parents, grandparents and etc.

Everything happens for growth and development.

Now let's take a young adult who dies and has forgotten more of where they came from. There will be others and crossed over relatives to help in the transition. This may take a little time after death as strong-minded persons will have to settle down and take direction from others. Get a sense of humor if you are strong minded, no right or wrong but it will come in handy later. My daughter died at 31 and I believe this was her. She had all her life de ja vu, so I thought she would have an easy time in spirit world but I had a dream six months after she died and she said she was having a hard time adjusting there. She likely had some unfinished business on earth that she was processing. She taught me a lot about death and dying and she was very positive about teaching others. She spent eleven years in philosophy classes, so maybe she just wanted to think she already knew it. This is not a criticism but an example of there is so much to know that no one knows much. She had cancer off and on for sixteen years and what a character. She would tell me each time the cancer (a different one) was there that, I was to get with the program and for three times; "this is not about death and dying as God was not finished with her on planet earth yet". Then the last cancer was usually found in children and she said, "isn't it just like me to get childhood cancer and this is about death and dying". She knew it was time to go home and she did it with grace. The week before she died, she said, "Mom I know daughter are not supposed to die before Mom's but remember I will not be far away as I will be right on your shoulder," as she pointed to my shoulder. This came in handy when she died and I tried to console her two sons by reminding them of what Mom said.

I first said, "Where is God?" They replied everywhere. "What is God?" They replied spirit. "What is Mommy now? "They replied spirit. They were present a week ago and heard their mom say that she was not far away but, on my shoulder, so I repeated that if spirit is everywhere than Mom is on their shoulder as well as mine. You should have seen the transition in their eyes, they went from not knowing what to feel to a spark in their eyes. You get what you need!

She had a lot of de ja vu from a very young age. It was likely the beginning point for a deeper look into metaphysics for me. I am glad that I never squashed it in her and tried to learn about it so to understand it. It comes from a French word, for already seen, our road map, our life chart or remembering before birth. It is also thought to be a tapping into the Akaskic Records of life.

The tree of life is mentioned in the bible and is likely the same reference for. It is the record of all knowing. All of life is in there. As a little girl she would say, "I remember this" and we would not have ever been there. At 14 years of age, she and I were at the Corn Palace in S. Dakota and when we got to the door about to go in, she stopped short and I looked at her startled look on her face and said, "de ja vu" and she said "yes" We crossed the street to the doll museum and the same thing happen but she was a little less startled. Before she died at 31, I asked her if de ja vu has increased and she said, "yes, but she paid less attention to it". I told her that I thought she would pay more attention but she just seemed to not want to talk about it. It may have been helping her process death as she did it so well. This was November and she died February 8th 2003.

The meaning of life is to become all you can become or another way to put it is to advance our souls. It is not about doing it is about being. We get caught up in materialism in our culture and may never get beyond that in this life time but do not worry, there is a next time. If we move beyond materialism then we will likely start to think of spiritualism. Body, mind and soul approach.

Now let's take the death of an elderly. The soul of the elderly dying has a chance to go where it needs to go if the person knows or remembers life is eternal and will take with them what they believe. That is why it is important to process the soul or spirituality. You are what you believe.

The person will go to the place that is comfortable and familiar to them, they will be met by others to help them feel comfortable with the process. It takes some dedication to our spiritual life to understand and be comfortable. I believe that the study of all religion is very, very helpful as Christianity has lost the spirituality more in favor of dogma, rules and regulations. Some churches even became more about money and the material just as the individual did. And why not the churches are just a group of individuals. The principle is the whole is only as good as its weakest link. We all need to go into the unknown rather than stay in our comfort zone. If you are wanting a starting place, read a book on near death experiences of child. It will help because as we know children usually say it like it is through their innocents. "Come as a little child", is the innocents and curiosity; traits of children. Never kill the child in you. Try to get to a place where death is not possible. You will likely conclude that all you have been taught in the fear of death and dying is not true. Change the thinking and process your fears. "I am not worthy" "I am not good enough" and "I have not done enough". God did not make junk. Say instead, "I am made of good stuff, God did not make junk." All experiences are teachers so learn to be all that you want to be, your higher self. Life is what we make it. Your fears are lies. My realizing that my feelings lie to me, that what I FEARED was not true or real was a very big eye opener. Thinking is a powerful tool. We spend too much time and energy wanting something without wanting to work for it.

You can go to church all your life and not be spiritual. Churches are about doing and not Being. We need to take time for the soul. I really do not think it is really an advancement of the soul as much as an understanding of the soul that we need. The soul already knows but we are not knowing about the soul. That is why it is said that everything we need is already inside us. I learned how to express what I feel is happening when I am counseling and I know I have gotten out of the way so spirit or my higher self is speaking. I am very aware when this is happening now. I am in God and God is in me or spirit or energy and etc. At first this may sound like blasphemy until you realize that the bible is always referring to inside us. Jesus always thought we would do greater things than he did but we are slow in the making. Actually, we have regressed in many ways from Jesus's time. It is mind boggling for me that we let ourselves become so primitive. It is high on life when you discover who and what God and you are. It is ecstasy. Start with love vs fear issues. Life is eternal. What does this mean? Think for yourself; no right or wrong; good or bad; just personally you. The church is a good foundation but do not live in the foundation forever, build your personal house. It took me 15 years to leave the church even though I knew I was not learning anything new. How long do you want to hear the same old same old? It does not make for growth of the soul. What really happen was on a Good Friday, I came home and wrote the sermon that was preached over and the light bulb went off and I knew I needed to go off to the forest alone for the rest of my building of my beliefs and spiritual home.

The Hindu beliefs include the idea that there are four stages of development in life. One as a student, next community, then going off by oneself or to the forest and the last is the wandering sage. I believe I am ready for the wandering sage. I like the wandering sage because to me it represents the freedom that you have earned. Yes, I do mean earned. It is a lot of effort that should go into life for it to have meaning. In church you remain the student and maybe community somewhat. I say somewhat as it is not about doing as much as being. I believe that in this stage of community it is more about defining a self as opposed to the others but with the help of the others. As your journey is about you. The need for approval keeps us stuck in doing. If I have been given talents, I need to use them but not for approval but in recognition for the need in the community. That way I am doing the right thing for the right reason. When is helping hurting should be a consideration. With all our laws and regulations, we have taken responsibility away from others. It leaves us victims rather than partners.

There is no punishment to death. Yes, your life will pass before you but it will be non-judgmental. The purpose of this passing before you is to let you see where you really are in the process of knowing and awareness. It will be comfort zone. You will except what is and it is that simple. I had my life pass before me and I was not in stress but was in bed awake. I was in the Alpha brain wave state or meditation stage. I sometimes rebel against being me. So

God shows me the results of being me. This may sound strange but it is the best explanation I have and it is strange to me also. God is unconditional love so why would our creator want to punish you for being you; that which he created. It would be punishing himself.

This brings me to another question; how can you punish spirit or energy? You die and you are now energy. You are now part of the whole. (You always are but you may not know that yet) Would you punish your hand because it did wrong? (Human's might come to think of it) Let's take the hand and correct what is wrong. Correcting what was wrong stays with you and maybe you will not want to repeat it. God does not humiliate you for that is not a feeling of God. We humiliate ourselves out of guilt. Guilt is not of God. You are choosing guilt. God is not human and does not have human emotions. That is why he does not punish, humiliate or produce guilt.

You bring to yourself what you believe. So bring to yourself a change in thinking and you will likely see change in your experiences.

God does not force you to know what you are not ready to know. That is why it is so important to be open to change and new learning or remembering. If our spirit is part of the whole and isn't into the emotions and is pure love, the feeling of the spirit or soul is love, joy, and ecstasy. Ecstasy here is rapture or high on Being. That high when you discover your truth. You know the bible says that the angel rejoices when you turn your life around or seek the truth. It is that kind of joy.

In the born-again experience there is a new found ecstasy or passion for Christ. Many get stuck there as they want it to last forever but growth would not be forthcoming if we stay there. It is a passion for the truth. Now keep the passion as a motivator to do the hard work ahead. The born-again experience is just the beginning for connecting to pure love, spirit, or God and you. It is now time for the personal understanding and awareness.

I say hard work ahead but really it is not necessary as it does not really matter if you go anywhere or not. It is all up to you and God has no preference. You have eternity to go where you want to go. This is not a race or competition as those are emotional concept which are not of God. It is ok to do your best or pull out of you what is already there. That potential or possibilities that you possess so it is not about anyone else. Do no comparison except with self. Be motivated by finding out what your capable of and uncover the mysteries of the universe. That is what drives me; the unknown. It is a process and we are all part of the process and journey. We are all one as we cannot do it without each other. Our differences are our beauty, for if we do not know this, we cannot know that. Differentness gives us choices. So figuring out our choices is the hard work that I was referring too. This is the process of knowing you and your journey, it is about you.

Get rid of a punishing God. Spirit is unconditional love and wants the best for you as you should want for yourself.

Death and dying issues are sometimes about cause and effect. There is the idea that we are all committing suicide one way or another. If we are body, mind and spirit then what are we doing to insure that we are taking care of all these aspects. Some over eat, others drink the wrong beverages, some smoke, some think the answer to everything is a pill that has worse side effects than the disorder that it is taken for, and fear in and of itself can cause death, by causing all sorts of physical issues.

This is a good place to talk about being still as in cause and effect. After death thinking is different It is all telepathy. You do not need a voice but you need a mind that know how to be still. How are you going to know how to be still in the mind if you have no concept of it in life.

Now see why you have many lives. So thinking is the powerhouse. Thinking goes with you and is the powerhouse in death. So having some control over thinking in life will help in death so that you have a chance to go where you need to go just like in life. You may want to practice going nowhere as it may be the best to pause after death and get your bearings. Be wide eyed and excited as everything is different and you have been there before. No thing to fear but fear itself.

Thinking is instant after death and spirit body is light as opposed to our heavy human body and moving around is instant. It is not right or wrong to be all over the place but it would get tiresome after a while, so a while for some maybe years, months, or days as time is an earthly concept. No time in spirit world. As I told my grandson's when their mother died that she could be on my shoulder and their shoulder at the same time, spirit can also be everywhere as God is at once. Hard to wrap you mind around? Yes," but there are more mysteries in this world than your philosophy books state," said Shakespeare. (paraphrased) A thousand years is but a day in spirit world.

Just think about thinking when you die as the instant you want to think of something it is there.

So want all the many things you want until you do not want them anymore. You will change your thinking in spirit world as you do on earth. Even jet setting gets boring after a while and people with money are not that happy, because it's not about having enough. It's about where we are in our growth and development. It is about going inside, money and things are outside. Who are you, what do you want to be and how to get there?

After you die is a lot like before you die in thinking. Rather, what you were thinking goes with you. The stage you are at is the stage you will be at in death.

Did I tell you when my life passed before me it was apparently boring because I remembered say, "Ok ok, let's get on with it." This sounds very rude but I am not a rude person, so I guess the remembering was just routine for me to the point that I already knew all this. We are remembering not learning really. One other reflection was that it was all good or positive. My take on good is that we take away only our growth and development, not how we got there. I remember when it was over laughing and thinking I was a little impatient with it all. The nice feeling left me to believe that I was just being me and patience may not be one of my strongest points. I felt loved all the time it was happening. This was about 1975 and I was about 37. Time lines I believe are important in our lives and journaling is a part of it. Now yours and mine will be different and should be. We need to validate the differentness as beauty. Patience is one of the areas that I have worked hard on in this life time, as I was a perfectionist and it was always wanting a fair just world. Get real Lois has been my journey.

Spirit world is different but not so different from our earth world except that space and time are non-existing. Let us take a minute and look how driven we are in earth world with time. Work, play, sleep and ageing are time oriented. Nine to five, weekends, darkness, and oldness are all gaged by time. Now take time away and you will create a stressless beingness. It is what makes for the peace that passes all understanding. We think we want the day to ourselves and half through the day we have to be with other or have something to do. We are driven by time and accomplishments. Learning to be alone with oneself is just that, you need to like your own company enough to like being alone. It is a must lesson sooner or later. I am a real people person so this was a big lesson for me. Now I may like being alone too much. I golf, ski and do much alone and love it. My first thought in being alone was that I am in charge of my own happiness and no one else is. We look to others for our happiness culturally so until we go inside, happiness is fleeting. We get temporary happiness from others and things. So heaven is stressless. Earth life can be also if you go inside and not be dictated to by the outside or others. Life is what you make it! Choose to make it less stressful. It is said that up to 95% of our dis-eases are stress related, so the need to reduce stress is important.

Thinking in the positive helps keep us motivated in issues. It would not be that bad things would not happen, it would be that we would see them, find the lesson and move ahead with change and fix them so as not to have to revisit them time and again. This would be all positive and less stressful. I believe we have challenges not problems. Now the word we use either has positive power or keeps us stuck. More motivated, freer to fine better solutions. Negativity makes us fearful. You bring to you what you fear. It is a blocker of free-flowing ideas. The old test taking technique was to take a deep breath and relax, then thinking will be forth coming. You already knew the answer. Relaxing will take fear out of play in decision making.

Love is all there is and it is what you take with you when you die, all the love you have shown others, places, animals and planet earth. Real love conquers all. The driving force should be love in our culture instead of everyone for their selves. It helps if you see everyone as one in that they are your sister or brothers. Ask yourself in situations, "What does love look like?" Yes, there is tough love but even that is in everyone's best interest.

ENDNOTE